Service- and Component-based development

The Addison-Wesley Component Software Series

Clemens Szyperski, Series Editor

The Addison-Wesley Component Software Series collects key contributions that help architects, CTOs, project managers, technologists, component developers, component assemblers, and system integrators to embrace and understand the diverse field of component software. Taking its ingredients from the core areas of object technology, software architecture, software process management, and others, component software as a discipline is a unique synthesis. At the intersection of technology and market forces, the series covers the concepts of component software and the business case, tried and tested methods and processes, practical success stories, and lessons learned, current technologies, boundary integration technologies, leading commercial component products, and their backing business modes.

Publications in the series are selected based on both their applicability and their visionary strength, yielding both immediate and long-term value for the reader.

P. Allen, *Realizing eBusiness with Components*

C. Atkinson, *Component-based Product Line Engineering with UML*

J. Cheeseman and J. Daniels, *UML Components: A Simple Process For Specifying Component-based Software*

K. Whitehead, *Component-based Development: Principals and Planning for Business Systems*

C. Szyperski, *Component Software: Beyond Object-oriented Programming*

Service- and Component-based development

USING SELECT PERSPECTIVE™ AND UML

HEDLEY APPERLY, RALPH HOFMAN, STEVE LATCHEM, BARRY MAYBANK,
BARRY MCGIBBON, DAVID PIPER, CHRIS SIMONS

Addison-Wesley

An imprint of **PEARSON EDUCATION**

London · Boston · Indianapolis · New York · Mexico City · Toronto · Sydney · Tokyo · Singapore
Hong Kong · Cape Town · New Delhi · Madrid · Paris · Amersterdam · Munich · Milan · Stockholm

PEARSON EDUCATION LIMITED

Head Office:
Edinburgh Gate
Harlow CM20 2JE
Tel: +44 (0)1279 623623
Fax: +44 (0)1279 431059

London Office:
128 Long Acre
London WC2E 9AN
Tel: +44 (0)20 7447 2000
Fax: +44 (0)20 7447 2170
Website: www.it-minds.com
www.awprofessional.com

First published in Great Britain in 2003

© Aonix Corporation 2003

The rights of Hedley Apperly, Ralph Hofman, Steve Latchem, Barry Maybank, Barry McGibbon, David Piper, and Chris Simons to be identified as the Authors of this Work have been asserted by them in accordance with the Copyright, Designs and Patents Act 1988.

ISBN 0 321 15985 3

British Library Cataloguing in Publication Data
A CIP catalogue record for this book can be obtained from the British Library

Library of Congress Cataloging in Publication Data
Applied for.

10 9 8 7 6 5 4 3 2 1

Typeset by Pantek Arts Ltd, Maidstone, Kent
Printed and bound in the UK by Biddles Ltd of Guildford and King's Lynn

The Publisher's policy is to use paper manufactured from sustainable forests.

Copyright

Contents

Foreword

by David Sprott
www.CBDiForum.com, County Cork, Ireland

In the latter half of the 1990s we set out a far-reaching vision for the software industry. We said then that the software crisis would only be resolved by radical re-engineering of customary practices to create formal separation between units of software and to embrace the concepts of componentization.

We suggested that all types of software organization need to adopt practices that are well understood in the automotive, electronics or airline industries, where pre-prepared parts are routinely and widely traded and reused in order to achieve economies of scale, faster production and crucially higher quality. Closer to home, it is useful to examine the personal computer industry, which is highly analogous to the software industry. Here, large numbers of components implemented in different technologies provide services that operate in collaboration using agreed architectures, bus structures and protocols, with the highest level of component independence. Furthermore, there is a thriving market in components that are sourced on the basis of quality and cost criteria. Component upgrades happen routinely in concert with, or independently of, other components, without trauma because the service contracts and implementation dependencies are thoroughly specified and managed. There is no reason why a similar position in the software environment cannot be achieved.

The componentized software organization will have established an environment where custom solutions can be delivered by acquiring and reusing pre-existing components or services, with obvious advantages in cost and time. Today we have much of the technology base that is needed to support a componentized software world. The standards and protocols have been developed that have been embraced by tools vendors to provide a rich environment for component-based software approaches. And the advances in component-based technology continue apace, as support for service-oriented architectures rapidly matures, providing specialization of component-based interfaces with higher-order standards for self description, discovery and consumption.

When we set out the original vision, we recognized that for the software industry this would be a journey that would take some considerable time. While specific technologies may be adopted quickly, practices and processes are deeply embedded in the culture of IT organizations and take considerable time to change. Widespread componentization can have profound impacts on conventional organizations, requiring new roles and responsibilities, as well as elimination of others, and new external relationships to be managed. New approaches to architecture are also necessary, which has a profound impact on the entire software life cycle. It is relatively easy to embrace the component technologies, but it does take concerted effort to implement matching processes, which is where the real benefits come from.

The original Select Perspective was the first clear articulation of how to develop component-based systems for business enterprises. This new Select Perspective represents a considerable advance on earlier thinking and provides a maturity of guidance that is clearly based on deep and extensive practical experience. Five years ago, we were focused on techniques and development processes, with a strong emphasis on forward engineering. Today, the new Select Perspective provides detailed advice on how to achieve the real business benefits that come from a mature software delivery process that is predicated on the managed collaboration of supply, management and consumption activities.

Everyone involved in delivering and using enterprise-level software, whether as end-user or vendor, needs to embrace the vision that software must be delivered with a level of process management that is customary in other high-tech industries. The entire software industry and its customers need to adopt standards, practices and processes that enable sophisticated software systems to be built and crucially continuously evolved, in much the same way that an automobile or personal computer is built from parts from different manufacturers. As they say, we have the technology, but with the Select Perspective we also now have the practical, experience-based process that is essential to achieving the component-based vision.

About the authors

Hedley Apperly

Job title: Vice President Product Marketing and Development, Aonix.
Resumé: Hedley Apperly has graduate and postgraduate qualifications in production engineering, business computing and strategic marketing. His 19 years experience in IT, have focused on the design and development of relational, object-oriented and component-bases systems. He is also a committee member of the British Computer Societies (BCS), Object-Oriented Programming and Systems (OOPS) specialist group. As well as his involvement in *Component Based Development for Enterprise Systems*, published by Cambridge University Press, Hedley co-authored *Component Based Software Engineering; Putting the Pieces Together*, published by Addison-Wesley. He is a member of the Chartered Institute of Marketing (MCIM), and with Aonix is responsible for the Select Business Solutions strategy and product direction.

Ralph Hofman

Job title: Manager Services (Benelux), Aonix.
Resumé : Ralph Hofman studied computer science at the University of Twente in the Netherlands. He started working as a consultant and went on to manage a methods and tools department in a major international bank. Ralph has acquired a great deal of experience in the organizational aspects of implementing methods and tools in large companies. He is currently responsible for consultancy and services in the Benelux countries.

Steve Latchem

Job title: Vice President Professional Services, Aonix.
Resumé : Steve Latchem has held positions in large consultancy groups and IT departments ranging from business analyst to object-oriented consultant, architect and project manager. Steve now directs the global professional services

group. Steve collaborated on *AntiPatterns: Refactoring Software & Projects in Crisis* (1998, Wiley) and co-authored *Component Based Software Engineering; Putting the Pieces Together* (1999, Addison-Wesley.)

Barry Maybank

Job title: Principal Consultant, Aonix.
Resumé: Barry Maybank has been engineer, designer and architect within consultancy groups, IT product companies and engineering companies over the last 17 years.

Barry McGibbon

Job title: Associate Consultant, Aonix.
Resumé: Barry McGibbon has worked in the IT industry since 1967 and has held senior management positions with leading computing services providers. He has been involved in many component-based and e-business initiatives for significant organizations in the UK and Europe. As well as being a frequent contributor to major journals, he is author of *Managing Your Move to Object Technology* (1997, SIGS Books), and co-author of *Component Based Software Engineering* (1999, Addison-Wesley), and *UML Xtra-Light* (2002, Cambridge University Press.) Barry is Technical Chair for Europe's largest CBD/OO conference and a series editor for Cambridge University Press.

David Piper

Job title: Principal Consultant, Aonix.
Resumé: David Piper, has been a professional consultant for over 20 years within manufacturing, financial services and IT/business management consultancy with roles ranging from analyst to quality assurance manager and project manager.

Chris Simons

Job title: Senior Consultant, Aonix.
Resumé: Christopher Simons has been involved in real-time, defence, retail, public-sector and finance domains, with roles ranging from software engineer, and lead analyst to technical architect. He has also taught object-orientation and development processes at various universities as a visiting lecturer.

About the organization

Aonix

Aonix, a member of the Gores Technology Group, is an international software company with more than 35,000 installations and half a million users worldwide, including a significant share of the Global 1000. The company's mission is to improve customers' productivity by providing comprehensive solutions consisting of robust tools and services for business- and mission-critical software development, deployment, component and information management.

Aonix comprises three divisions: Enterprise Business Intelligence Solutions (eBIS); Critical Development Solutions (CDS); and Select Business Solutions (SBS.)

The eBIS division provides products and services designed to dramatically simplify access and analysis of mainframe data. eBIS makes critical data available universally through a variety of desktop clients, including PCs and web browsers, and enables users to focus more readily on achieving their business goals. Proven, flexible architecture and high-performance solutions are the hallmarks of eBIS' rapid application development and enterprise reporting offerings. eBIS products include Nomad® and UltraQuest Reporter™.

CDS products support the highest critical levels of software design. Aonix development tools cover a full range of real-time development requirements for hard real-time/deeply embedded systems, safety-critical development, and 'soft' real-time networked applications. The CDS division produces Software through Pictures® (StP), Architecture Component Development® (ACD), TeleUSE™, ObjectAda™, AdaWorld® and Raven™.

Select Business Solutions

For more than 10 years, Select has created a successful track record with tool and process solutions that have evolved based upon input from talented developers, a vast customer base and extensive market research. These solutions are primarily focused on business-critical application development, deployment and management. The technology behind Select is continually recognized as being innovative, ensuring that customers' demands are met to the fullest satisfaction. It is this three-way focus on development, customers, and emerging markets that makes Select Business Solutions a leader in its field.

The Select Business Solutions division of Aonix provides a comprehensive suite of business software development solutions, comprising Select Component Factory™, Select Enterprise®, Select Component Architect™, Select Process Director™, Select Reviewer™, Select JSync™, Select VBSync™, Select C++Sync™ and Select C#Sync™. These tools are supported by a full complement of professional services in addition to the component-based development methodology described in this book, Select Perspective™.

Preface

What this book is about

This book is about software development. It presents approaches and practices for the construction of software systems using a component-based approach. It details the key workflows for a modern approach to supplying, managing, and consuming software assets that meets the needs of the stakeholders of the business. Above all, this book is based on a proven, pragmatic approach to delivering successful software solutions in a wide variety of contexts: industry, scale, maturity. This approach is called Select Perspective™.

The approaches presented here were developed over many years at Select Business Solutions (SBS),[1] a division of Aonix. All the authors are leading experts involved in working with SBS customer teams worldwide to develop and deliver successful solutions. These solutions were built within many different types of businesss, covering such diverse sectors as financial services, call center operations, internet publishing, retail, manufacturing, and utility services. The team sizes ranged from a few developers to large globally distributed teams, all with different skill levels. This has made Select Perspective fit for real-world solution delivery.

Select Perspective is a blend of approaches from several object-oriented methods, improved and adapted to meet the new demands of component-based development and web services. It uses the Unified Modeling Language (UML) to communicate the designs, structures, and blueprints across all the roles involved in today's software development.

In contrast to those development approaches that are mainly concerned with the activities and tasks that often result in volumes of documents but do not produce meaningful deliverables, Select Perspective defines a small set of key deliverables and identifies the activities and tasks to produce them. If a particular diagram was not necessary to a particular solution then it is not produced.

---

1. Previously known as Select Software Tools Ltd.

The structure of this book

This book has eleven main chapters that cover the major topics of component-based development (CBD) using the Select Perspective. After the overview and introduction chapters are three key chapters covering the supply–manage–consume life cycle. These chapters detail the workflows, processes, and activities that ensure successful delivery of solutions. Although they are closely related, each chapter can be studied separately. The remaining chapters cover supporting material referred to in the main supply–manage–consume chapters, such as techniques and deliverables.

Chapter 1, *Introduction to contemporary software development*, outlines the experiences you need to derive real business benefits from using software components and services. It also shows how the component-based approach is similar to the scenario of building a house.

Chapter 2, *Overview of Select Perspective*, provides a description of the development life cycle for component-based solutions, outlines the business benefits of adopting this approach, and lays out the principles behind the method. It gives an introduction to supply–manage–consume workflows.

Chapter 3, *Supply*, discusses the issues surrounding the reuse/rent/buy/build debate for the supply of components and services, such as those provided by web services. It presents the detail on the tasks and activities for delivering components.

Chapter 4, *Manage*, shows how reusing components is more than simply storing them in a library and providing a catalog. This involves strategies for acquisition, certification, classification, and publishing of components, as well as success in locating and retrieving those components.

Chapter 5, *Consume*, forms an umbrella process for all those activities that focus on the project-based delivery of business solutions: business alignment, business architecture, technical architecture, solution delivery, solution rollout, maintenance and support. Each section describes these major processes in detail, and within this framework Select Perspective fully supports the concepts of incremental working and iteration.

Chapter 6, *Data architecture*, details the approach to handling the complexities of storing and managing data. It discusses the different approaches to data migrations and shows how data components provide a flexible and adaptable way to handle the information used by the solution.

Chapter 7, *Project management*, outlines core features of Select Perspective that address the issues that frequently arise in projects. These core features include use case driven, iterative working, incremental working, parallel working, and active support for different project types.

Chapter 8, *Roles*, list the skills and responsibilities for those roles that are special to the component-development approach as well as common roles where new skills are needed.

Chapter 9, *Techniques*, focuses on techniques that are special to the component-development approach.

Chapter 10, *Deliverables*, covers the many products produced during a CBD project, some of which are common to all types of software development project.

Chapter 11, *Tools*, provides details of the tools that support the component-based development approach with examples from the Select Business Solutions product range.

Who should read this book

Select Perspective is a pragmatic, component-based software development process that can be implemented by all roles in software development. It includes the business people that specify, accept, verify and use software solutions. As such, every individual who is involved in the specification, acceptance, construction, testing, delivery or budgetary control of software solutions will gain from the experiences, examples, and process definitions in this book.

We recommend that individuals fulfilling any role in software development read the first two chapters of this book to understand the principles, drivers, and benefits of a component-based approach to software specification, construction, and delivery. To gain full value from the content, generic roles are described in this section, and the areas of the book that are most appropriate are described. All individuals can gain from our experience in all the chapters; however, particular chapters and workflows provide specific assistance, guidelines, and principles for particular roles.

Chief executives, senior technology executives, CIOs and CTOs

For executives involved in the management, control, and strategic direction setting for software development in their organizations, the supply–manage–consume model and principles described in the first few chapters will be of particular interest, together with the roles, techniques, deliverables and tools definitions. The remaining detailed workflow chapters and case study will then provide concrete examples and definitions to emphasize the impact of adopting these process and technology principles.

Project and program managers

To assess project and program team roles, skills, deliverables and use of tools, Chapters 8–11 will provide detailed definitions and relationships to the process workflows. The key chapter for you is the one on project management workflow (Chapter 7).

Business analysts

Chapter 5 has workflows that describe the alignment of requirements and business process models to the business and the development of the business architecture. This then follows through the consume workflows to the solution delivery and solution rollout workflows, which cover the design, development, testing, acceptance, and rollout of the software solution aligned to the business.

Software developers

Depending on the architectural layer in which you develop, i.e. solution (user interface and process control components) or business/infrastructure (business, data, legacy wrapping, COTS components), either the consume or supply workflows will provide the activities, dependencies, modeling deliverables, and techniques for you. For the more technically focused, the specific technical architecture workflow will add invaluable experience. Also, the component management workflow provides the mechanisms for publishing and reusing components and implementing the 'design by contract' paradigm.

Software designers

Similar to software developers, the applicable workflows depend on the architectural layer in which you design. Either the consume (user and process control layers) or supply (business/infrastructure component layer) workflows will provide the activities, dependencies, modeling deliverables, and techniques for you.

Software engineers and architects

In particular, the technical architecture workflow in Chapter 5 provides a unique model-centric approach to analysis, design, and implementation of technical architecture frameworks and the integration of these into business solutions. Depending on your architectural responsibility, i.e. solution or component development, Chapters 3 and 5 provide invaluable insight into the activities surrounding component-based design, testing and deployment. The component management workflow will help if you have any responsibility for reuse and/or maintenance and storage of your components.

Software testers and quality assurance analysts

Each of the workflows has elements of testing and accreditation; therefore, the supply, manage, and consume workflows detail the testing activities and dependencies. Furthermore, Chapters 8–10 provide detailed definitions of the outputs and various responsibilities.

Process owners

All of the workflow definition chapters will be of particular interest to you, with their detailed definitions of activities, dependencies and prerequisites. Definitions in Chapters 8–11 add the final pieces to refining your own processes to adopt component-based analysis, design, construction, testing, and deployment.

Computer science and software engineering academics/students

For any student, lecturer, or professor attending, teaching, or managing a computer science or software engineering course, all chapters of this book provide valuable, industry-proven processes, techniques and deliverables, which are critical to component-based analysis, design, development, testing, and deployment.

Acknowledgements

First, we would like to extend our greatest thanks to the customers of Select Software Tools, Princeton Softech and Aonix's Select Business Solutions division. Without their real projects with real business issues, budgets and timescales, none of the founding experience for the Select Perspective would exist. The consultants used in these projects were highly skilled but also used the experiences to continually refine the Select Perspective component and service-based development process. This is not insignificant, as the projects number more than 1,000 in North American, European (especially the UK and Benelux) and global organizations. To name all of the countries in which the Select Perspective has been tested and practised on customer projects would fill the page, but the reach can be indicated by just a few: China, Australia, Brazil, Sweden, the Netherlands, Germany, England, the USA, Hong Kong and Poland.

Second, the authors would like to thank their respective employers over the period of Select Perspective evolution. The writing of this book took place under the management of Ashley Abdo, CEO and President of Aonix, to whom we are grateful for the gainful employment and unerring support.

Many more people and organizations have played a part in the development of Select Perspective and this book: the non-author (pre- and post-sales) consultants past and present, who all worked towards a common goal; the managers within Select Software Tools, Princeton Softech and Aonix, who supported and nurtured their staff; the staff in marketing, sales, software development and support, who all played a part in the development of the Select Perspective and this book; and the partner organizations and competitors, who helped to support good ideas and identify weaker alternatives, respectively.

We would also like to thank the various authors who helped to found the object-oriented and component/service-based movements. They have paved the way and sown many a useful seed.

Finally, and most importantly, we would like to thank our partners, parents, children, relatives and friends for their support, particularly when it may have appeared that we had our minds on different things. We care for you and appreciate the time you have allowed us to work on this book.

Introduction

Every business faces constant change, and these changes increase the pressure on IT development to deliver successful solutions. Changes to the business make new demands on IT developers to respond quickly to the opportunities or threats to the core business. Solution development is measured in weeks rather than months, which means that the development process must be responsive to the different needs of each project. This approach is known as *agile development*, of which eXtreme Programming [Beck] is a well-known example.

Changes in technology also increase the demands on the IT community. Many of these changes are improvements of an existing technology that requires a re-evaluation of current systems. Such re-evaluation can result in significant work in upgrading these systems, which can be mitigated by the development of adaptable systems, i.e. systems that have been designed for change.[1] The key to providing adaptable systems is *components*. Each component delivers a set of services published as clearly defined interfaces, behind which is the encapsulated behavior and information to support the required operations. Components are designed to be highly flexible, i.e. any changes are contained within the boundary of the component without affecting other components. Every attempt is made to minimize any dependency on the development or deployment environments, especially the user interface. The delivered solution is then an assembly of components that can be deployed in a number of combinations.

However, other technology changes involve a significant shift in technology; these are often called 'discontinuous innovations'. They have a new nature, which means they do not fit the 'old' way of building solutions; they demand new skills from the IT community, and they introduce new risks to development projects. An example of such a shift is the growth of web services. The term 'web service' has been coined to describe an application service that is accessible either publicly or privately using web-based protocols. At its simplest, a web service could be used to pass a single business document, such as a purchase order, between two companies. Web services can also be used for more

---

1. Older systems generally do not have this characteristic and need to be re-engineered to provide an adaptable solution (see 'Componentization of legacy systems' in Chapter 3)

complex interactions, such as processing a payment transaction, conducting a credit check or performing an insurance risk assessment. At the heart of web services are a number of standards aimed at enabling communication between software applications over the internet, e.g. SOAP, a mechanism for accessing service functionality using HTTP and eXtensible Markup Language (XML) schemata. These standards enable not just whole applications to be accessed but also individual application services, a concept that fits well with the evolution of application architecture towards components and services.

New technology cannot be ignored; it must be tackled. Developers must start the long journey to understand the technology, evaluate the benefits, assess the impact, prove the claims, and finally incorporate it into appropriate solutions. The map for such a journey is a defined *development process*. A process defines a way of working: a blueprint of workflows, steps, and tasks that shows how to deliver successful solutions in a number of different contexts. This blueprint must be sufficiently flexible to accommodate significant shifts in technology and yet provide the rigor required to support the complex business of developing solutions.

This book is about such a process: Select Perspective™

Select Perspective has had a long history. It first appeared in 1994 as a response to Select's visual modeling tool customers, who needed to establish a method of working in object-oriented technology. Their existing processes, which were usually based on structured techniques, did not seem to fit the new high-energy activities surrounding object-based development. Much of the early process was derived from the rapid application development (RAD) approach as published by the Dynamic Systems Development Method (DSDM) consortium.

However, Select Perspective was, and still is, different. From its early days Select Perspective, unlike many other processes, has had two key characteristics:

1. It is delivery-focused.
2. It has been tested, evolved, and proven on many projects.

The majority of software development processes are mainly concerned with the activities and tasks that often result in volumes of documents that capture facets of the problem and solution. Developers can get caught in cycles of activity that keep them busy but do not produce meaningful deliverables; you often hear of 'analysis paralysis'. The early authors of Select Perspective believed in defining a small set of key deliverables and identified the activities and tasks to produce them. If a particular diagram was not necessary to a particular solution then you did not produce it. This principle applies to Select Perspective to this day.

The second key characteristic of Select Perspective is that it is based on experience: experience gained by many Select staff working with customer teams to deliver successful solutions for different types of business in diverse business sectors. The development teams varied in numbers with each individual at a different skill level. This experience-based characteristic has made Select Perspective fit for real-world solution delivery.

Since 1994, Select Perspective has changed; it has had to evolve to cater for changes in the business and software development world. One of the first changes was to include architecture as a key part of the solution deliverables. This gave rise to the RAAD (rapid architected application development) approach, which enabled complex business applications to be built quickly while ensuring that the software architecture was fundamentally sound and scalable. Select Perspective became more powerful to handle these new deliverables, which defined the multi-tiered architecture and framework of modern distributed systems.

The second major and most significant change to Select Perspective started in 1997. This was the move to components. Object technology and object-based development became the preferred approach to delivering modern solutions, but some of the promised benefits were hard to realize. The major benefit that was the most difficult to realize was that of increased developer productivity through the reuse of objects. Objects are too fine-grained (small) for significant levels of reuse. Developers do use common framework objects such as GUI controls, but the major benefit is the reuse of business objects such as Product, Customer, and Order Capture. Today's programming languages now support component and service principles in response to these object-oriented issues.

Components are generally coarse-grained (large) encapsulations with more functionality than individual objects. A components publishes an interface that defines the services it offers, and the actual functions and data are provided as a black box: you know what it does, but not how it does it. Components may then capture business (or presentation) functionality and can then be reused in many different solutions. With this enforced separation of responsibilities between the interface (a contract) and the implementation, it becomes possible to have true concurrent development.

SBS knew that these benefits could be realized and encouraged its customers (and others in the industry) to make the move towards component-based development (CBD.) To make this move successful, Select Perspective needed to reflect the new development vision of the 'supply–manage–consume' model for CBD.

Based on our process development principles (delivery-focused, tested and proven) the Select staff started exploring and augmenting Select Perspective to provide a pragmatic CBD approach that met the needs of our customers.

This version of Select Perspective has evolved over many years through discussion, drafting, testing, and reviewing to arrive at its form today. It has been the work of many hours from a wide range of authors and reviewers drawing on their many years of experience. The result is a comprehensive and adaptive set of life cycle processes that define component-based development for a wide range of different project types.

Select Perspective is not finished; it will never be finished. Over the coming months and years it will change, adapt, and evolve as we and our customers tackle new project types, integrate new technology, overcome organizational changes, and meet the high expectations from business management to deliver solutions that are critical to the business.

This book is therefore a *snapshot* of Select Perspective as it is today, giving you an insight into the vast real-world experience that has been documented and evolved since 1994. We will continue to use your feedback to improve this contemporary software development process, keeping it relevant and useful, as it has always been.

As well as a snapshot in time, this book is also a *subset* of the extensive detail contained in Select Perspective. The full detail of the workflows, deliverables, etc. is to be found in our computer-based version, provided with Select Process Director tool (see Chapter 11.)

Introduction to contemporary software development

1

Although contemporary software development is founded upon a solid background of experience within the software industry, it is a relatively immature engineering science. It is our experience that successful processes need to be shared and evolved into best practices if more organizations are to succeed with component- and service-based development (CBD). The first problem is that software development organizations and information services (IS) departments are often in competition, with closely guarded proprietary processes. For example, if an IS manager fails to deliver a software system, one option may be to outsource the development wholesale. If you assume that the in-house and outsourced staff and development tools are equivalent, then the primary difference is the process followed to develop the software system.

In this chapter, we outline the experiences you need to derive real business benefits from using software components. Second, we explain the 'experience trap', which suggests that because components have evolved from object-orientation (OO), many so-called 'experts' take credit for their days in OO. Obviously previous design experience is invaluable, but you must understand that CBD is both a new perspective in software engineering and a tested solution in other engineering disciplines.

Many industries have evolved to use components over a long period of time, including manufacturing, electronics, construction, and automotive [D'Souza and Wills]. Most of you reading this book have been involved with the construction industry: either you live in a building, have made changes to a building, or in some cases been involved in construction. So a 'high-rise construction' scenario will therefore best describe the opportunities and problems inherent in component-based construction.

Basics of construction

Constructing a high-rise building can be decomposed into a set of very high-level steps. Table 1.1 shows a simplified life cycle. The general flow seems to be a standard waterfall development process [Bocij *et al.*], but we should bear in mind that increments and iteration will occur. For example, you may choose (or be forced) to occupy the lower-level floors before all of the construction has been completed, which maps to incremental development. Incremental development is a technique for identifying priorities and delivering high-priority items first. When building a high-rise office you may be happy to move staff into the building while a roof garden is being completed. The same is true for software, as you probably need input screens well before you need monthly reports. Iteration can be mapped to walls, as you usually start with bricks and come back to add a plaster coating, followed by paint or paper. This technique is termed 'additive', as a basic infrastructure is built upon. The infrastructure maps to software development as early versions of software are evolved over time.

We can continue this table to include the building maintenance, as shown in Table 1.2. These typical construction steps can easily be mapped to a traditional software development life cycle. Before we move on to a comparison of software components with high-rise construction components, it is useful to compare the processes for constructing both buildings and software (Table 1.3).

Table 1.1   Constructing a high-rise building

1	Analyze business/owner's processes
2	Define business/owner's requirements
3	Design building
4	Hire construction company
5	Lay foundation
6	Construct infrastructure
7	Build façade
8	Decorate
9	Occupy

Table 1.2   Maintaining a high-rise building

10	Remodel foyer
11	Build extension
12	Join two office blocks together

Table 1.3 Building software

Step	Construction phases	Software development life cycle phases
1	Analyze business/owner's processes	Model business processes
2	Define business/owner's requirements	Manage requirements
3	Design building	Model system design
4	Hire construction company	Select integrated development environment (IDE)
5	Lay foundations	Build database
6	Construct infrastructure	Build middleware
7	Build façade	Build client software
8	Decorate	Test
9	Occupy	rollout / deploy
10	Remodel foyer	Software maintenance
11	Build extension	System extension
12	Join two office blocks together	Merge systems

Mapping construction to software component development phases is somewhat straightforward, and you can see how increments and iterations map to the construction and software processes. We could also envisage a prototype of the building, perhaps even a scale model.

Componentization

Over the years, the construction industry has realized that it is not practical to build everything from scratch every time. Doors, windows, and bricks are all built off site, often by a different company or team. In most cases, standard construction components will fit the needs of the designer and builder. At other times, a new component will be specified and built to suit the specific needs of a single building. We assert that no industry can become componentized until it has successfully shown how to *consume, supply,* and *manage* components.

Consume

The basics of building a house map to the construction of a solution or application. The focus for this 'solution building' process [Allen and Frost] is provided by the customer or the business [Eles and Sims]. In the software engineering world, this is usually achieved by modeling your required business processes [Jacobson]. The contract between the customer and the designer can be achieved by documenting requirements or by reviewing the designs as they progress. Once solution design starts, components begin to have an impact. The group responsible for building solutions is actually consuming components. This highlights our first problem: not only is it important to stockpile the components ready for the construction process, but it is also important to design the solution using information about available components. The Select Perspective solution for the design of interacting components is based on the Unified Modeling Language (UML) and is described in Chapters 5 and 9. However, we believe that UML is even better for designing the internals of black-box components rather than designing static and dynamic relationships between components. For this very reason, we provide extensions to UML for component-based design. The challenge for the solution builder is to assemble a large system from components; to do this successfully, they will need information about the available software components or web services, their required interfaces, and their services/operations/methods.

The process of finding the right components is important to the architect and is usually termed *gap fulfillment* [Bellows]. The gap fulfillment process can have one of two outcomes: either an ideal (or similar) component is found and can be used, or no relevant component exists. This introduces new issues to the stockpiling process, because you may need to create a sub-project to build a specific component. This means that the stockpiling process is not just about static holding areas for built components but is also an enabling process. The real productivity benefits of CBD will only be realized by enabling parallel solution and component development, and this is achievable only with planning and design. For components that cannot be found, the stockpiling process needs to allow consumers to post a 'wanted' notice for others to respond to.

Once you use a component, whether off-the-shelf or bespoke,[1] you need a process for configuration management. New versions of a component may be provided that the solution builder may want to take advantage of. There needs to be a process to inform component consumers when updated components are added to the stockpile. The solution builder must be able to easily replace a component with a newer version of that component. This can be achieved, for example, if the solution builder is on a mailing list to receive notification when new component versions are stockpiled.

Table 1.4 shows the application development life cycle with these additional component-based steps. This table is again simplified, but it communicates the component considerations that improve the standard solution-building process. We can take this model one step further by considering the actual deployment of the components on the runtime environment. Typically, the particular computers on which the components run are called 'nodes' [UML 1.x], and mapping these nodes to the components allows us to manage the deployment configuration. This is particularly important when components are widely distributed across organizations and updates occur. To handle this complexity, the process should be enhanced to include deployment recording during the application rollout stage.

---

1. A term used to describe unique, specially developed components.

Table 1.4   Solution life cycle with CBSE

Step	Construction phases	Software development life cycle phases
1	Analyze process	Model business processes
2	Define requirements	Manage requirements
3	Design building	Model system design (components)
CBD	Find windows and doors	Gap fulfillment
CBD	Subcontract roof joists	New component specification
CBD	Design in windows	Component use
CBD	Get on mailing list	Get on mailing list
4	Hire construction company	Select integrated development environment (IDE)
5	Lay foundations	Build database (comp. assembly)
6	Construct framework	Build middleware (comp. assembly)
7	Build façade	Build client software (comp. assembly)
8	Decorate	Test
9	Move in	Rollout
CBD	New catalog	Receive notification, new component
CBD	Read catalog	Review new component
CBD	Update design	Update design
10	Remodel foyer	Maintenance
11	Build extension	Extension
12	Join office blocks together	Merge systems

This generally completes the steps in the solution-development process or, as we have called it, component consumption.

Supply

The component supplier is responsible for building completed components, usually to predefined component specifications. In the construction industry, for example, there are window supply companies whose sole source of revenue (and hopefully profit) is window manufacturing. Windows generally come in standard sizes, although builders can request special sizes and materials as described by a comprehensive specification. Roof joists are a good example of specified components that are often distinct to a particular building. Even with bespoke supplies, standards will be used to define basic interfaces. As well as the customer's component specification, there may be industry standards to apply. In the case of the high-rise building, there will be safety standards such as elevator standards, structural standards such as stress loading for girders, emergency standards such as fire exits, and materials standards. These standards map to the ideas of quality, performance, error handling, and technology standards in software components.

Applying similar logic to the discipline of CBD, the *component specification* may come from the component producer's desire to provide a generic component or the solution builder's specific needs, communicated via the specification. A component specification defines, as a minimum, the interfaces, services, parameters (plus descriptions of all three), required technology type, and business requirements for the component. The specification may also derive from an industry standard for component interaction or a component kit [D'Souza and Wills].

A component supplier starts by identifying the discrete requirements of the component specification. This is an important step in the supplier/consumer process, as the component specification forms the contractual expectations of both parties to the component-development process and final product. This approach is termed 'design by contract' [Meyer].

Starting with this specification and perhaps some component-specific use cases (defined in later chapters), the component supplier iteratively and comprehensively develops a design that satisfies the specification. Typically, the design and development of the internals of the component will be carried out using various techniques and documented using UML and object-oriented (OO) languages, or even plugging together smaller components. Tools for design and code generation may also be used. Testing, debugging, and compilation are generally applied. The important result, for the subject of this chapter, is the completed component.

A component typically has four levels of abstraction, as shown in Table 1.5. The component specification or 'façade' [Gamma *et al.*] includes the technology-independent definition of the component, as well as information to facilitate gap fulfillment. The minimum requirements for a component specification are defined above, and these form the binding contract between the supplier and consumer. Component management tools can help with this process, as well as ensuring that authority to proceed is granted.

Table 1.5 Component abstraction levels

1	Component specification
2	Component implementation
3	Component executable
4	Component deployment

The component specification is the primary reference resource used at design time. It has been our experience that component specifications change during the development life cycle. Therefore, component producers will generally develop multiple versions of a particular component.

A component implementation occurs when you decide on the language to use to develop the component. This defines the 'inside' of the component, with its internal parts and their collaborations. The implementation source code is typically what will be stored in a configuration management or version control system. By 'implementation' source code, we do not mean the formal OO 'implements' statement. We mean all of the source code for the component. Because a component specification can be implemented using more than one language, there is a 'one-to-many' relationship between a specification and an implementation: multiple versions of an implementation will occur during the course of the life cycle.

Finally. the component executable is the real 'pluggable' component or web service used in the assembly of the solution. Each executable/service may result in more than one version, and there may be more than one executable per implementation. This component executable is deployed on a number of nodes to provide services. In turn, all nodes need to be inventoried and tracked so that updates are managed and a stable production environment is maintained.

Accurate information about a component, such as its available interfaces and its services, needs to be published by the supplier. Most important in publishing the component is communicating the specification of the component and its interfaces with a focus on making the physical component available. Updates to software will occur, so new component versions will need to be published in the same manner as the original. As a component consumer, you may expect to receive the latest catalogs and updates, and perhaps even be informed about product recalls.

Building software components is similar to any company that builds windows or doors for the construction industry. A window can be viewed as a black-box component. The high-rise contractor will not need to know the size of each pane of glass or the size of nails used in the windows' construction. The contractor does need to know the outer size (say 3×2), the thickness, and information about its functionality. The functionality information is required because the builder's component specification, acquired from the developer of the high-rise building, probably in consultation with an engineer, forms the contract between the developer, the contractor and the subcontractor. Double- or single-glazed, top or side opening, and tinted windows are all examples of functions of a window that do not relate directly to the interface. In the case of a window, the interface is where it touches the brickwork, i.e. the 3×2 hole in the wall.

You can see from this short discussion that you need more than just a single interface specification to find and use a component. A degree of functionality and how it is to be achieved also needs to be communicated as part of the component specification.

Manage

The third high-level role in general component-based engineering is *component management*. Previously, we have referred to a stockpile of components; this describes exactly a typical *component library*.

A component library is similar to a builder's yard or warehouse; both environments are where construction companies – software or building – order and purchase their components. Component suppliers publish their components in both settings. Builders' yards and warehouses are staging areas between suppliers and consumers; they serve as the 'middle men' for the construction component businesses. In the construction world, there are various levels of interacting component store as in Figure 1.1. The top level is the warehouse of the component supplier. Component suppliers that assemble windows will typically have a central store that is used to supply all the builder's merchants. The builder's merchants will have their own warehouses, which are closer to the construction sites and will typically service many construction companies. In this example, a third level would be the builder's yard for the construction company. This stock will consist of newly acquired components and components available from previous jobs. Therefore, construction companies develop an inventory from previous contract assignments and attempt to use existing stock before they purchase more, and before building it themselves. This technique is typically termed 'reuse before you buy, and before you build'. However, modern construction and manufacturing companies are increasingly moving towards the just-in-time (JIT) approach to component supply. In this approach, the components are moved directly from the supplier to the construction/assembly site with a minimal inventory store. Software components do not suffer from the same capacity issues as there is little or no reproduction cost, although the ideas are similar.

Warehouse organization is important, as cataloguing helps to manage and locate components. The standard way to support multiple sites and interacting levels of warehouses is usually an integrated set of component repositories or catalogs.

Figure 1.1
Interacting
component stores
in the construction
industry

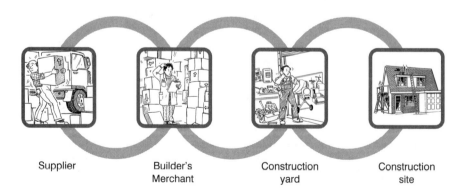

Supplier   Builder's   Construction   Construction
                  Merchant   yard   site

Component suppliers do not simply ship new components to the builder's yard. Effective builders' yards employ a receivable-goods clerk, who assures that the products arriving at the warehouse are the correct items and of acceptable quality. If the components do not meet quality standards, the shipment is rejected. If the components comply with the standards, the clerk certifies the components for component consumers and end-users of the warehouse to purchase the stock.

New components are the other key factor for component librarians, as they may not always arrive fully documented or designed. Generally, new components require extra information to be recorded if the components are to be easily retrieved and used. Software components especially require information, often referred to as *meta-data*, which includes technology type, features provided, where to get support, examples of use, help files, and installation procedures.

It is worth clarifying here that components are typically physical items but that in the construction industry pure services may also be available. In fact, you may never buy a crane, but you would typically use crane services over time. For this reason, components and services have been used somewhat interchangeably in this chapter. The differences are clarified in following chapters.

Conclusion

The development and maintenance of software components is similar to other engineering endeavors, especially the analysis, design, component warehousing, construction, and maintenance of high-rise buildings. Constructing from components is more complex than building from scratch. The transition from building the same sets of software products repeatedly to componentization demands new and existing roles; it can be seen as requiring a cultural shift. This is not really the case.

Building systems from components is a natural evolution from existing methods and can always be related to other industries. Car manufacture, electronics, construction, and many other industries' engineering disciplines have adopted componentization because of economics and matured into more productive and profitable industries.

CBD techniques apply equally to small teams and large inter-enterprise CBD endeavors. The rest of this book enlarges this underlying concept and provides the detail of the Select Perspective, which is a set of CBD best practices focused on the software development industry.

Component benefits

For any new approach to be adopted there must be tangible benefits. The benefits of component-based development have evolved over time and fall into a number of categories: technical, business, and economic.

Technical benefits

The technical benefit is 'simplicity through abstraction'. This springs from the underlying nature of a component: its *boundary* (e.g. the encapsulated functionality, the service contract). A strong boundary encloses complexity. If there are complex functions to perform such as tax calculations, then these can be enclosed within the boundary of a tax component. Component developers focus solely on the tax formulae, rules, etc. Focus gives more benefit than a small scope of interest; it also increases productivity by ignoring irrelevant topics.

Containment of complexity also leads to *assembly of solutions* rather than full-scale development. Components can be plugged together to assemble complex functionality quickly and may be substituted later if necessary; this is often called 'plugability'.

When you have a clear delineation of a boundary and can specify the services – the component with its interface contract – then it becomes possible to distribute the work necessary to construct the component itself. This may be distributed within the organization or outsourced to another reliable partner. Maintenance for the component may then be the responsibility of the supplier – the trusted partner – or may be undertaken by the component consumers themselves.

As the supplier improves the component, say including up-to-date tax rules, the consumers of the component benefit from these upgrades when and if applicable.

Business benefits

Massive parallel development and the capability to outsource development results in faster development cycles – you simply get there quicker. There is more work perhaps, in locating or buying suitable components and services, and certainly more effort in testing and integrating these into a possible solution. But this effort is less than building everything from scratch. Solution delivery becomes more assembly, less development, and new recruits to the team can be productive earlier as they have 'building blocks' of components readily available. Also in the case of our tax component, tax experts will work with the component developers to encode their rare expertise into the final component; we don't all have to become taxation experts!

Economic benefits

In the language of the markets, a commodity is any item that may be freely bought and sold; the key phrase here is 'freely bought and sold'. Components used to be restricted to the confines of an organization. Now there are marketplaces and brokers that buy and sell components and services. These market forces are lowering costs through multiple sales and raising the quality of the supplied component as greater numbers of buyers reuse it within their solutions. As a result, it has become increasingly uneconomic to build a complete system from scratch.

Overview of Select Perspective 2

Select Perspective is a comprehensive development life cycle for component-based solutions that supports parallel development activities in order to reduce the time-to-market for your product or solution. Unlike other software development processes, Select Perspective is focused on a small number of key deliverables within an organizational framework of suppliers and consumers of solution-driven components.

Component-based design and development has become *the* contemporary approach for delivering solutions that meet the needs of modern businesses. This is no accident. Components and services offer important business, technical, and economic benefits for any organization, whether large or small. Select Perspective supports component-based development.

To realize these benefits, it is critical that your software development life cycle is designed to support the contemporary approach. While it may be tempting to consider components and services simply as a software construction technique and modify any existing processes – assuming you have them defined – this will not leverage the power of components and services.

Key to this power is the containment of complexity. Components have a strong boundary that is protected during the many stages of development, i.e. analysis, design, construction, testing and deployment. This encourages a development process that supports parallel development, including activities distributed across multiple sites.

Select Perspective supports parallel and distributed development. Parallel development leads to new organizational dynamics: the interaction between suppliers and consumers of components. Solution builders consume components and services that come from a number of sources: constructed by other project teams, reused corporate software assets, provided by component brokers, or supplied by third-party partners. Select Perspective supports the supplier and consumer communities.

Component-based development

Components have numerous and varied descriptions. Despite this perceived confusion, there is a small set of characteristics that component developers agree upon:

- Components are units of deployment, i.e. they run within computer systems.
- Each component has a published interface that defines its responsibilities as a set of services, e.g. knowing customers' personal details.
- Components interact with other components according to defined communications standards.
- Components are assembled to realize solutions.

Component-based development (CBD) combines the construction and testing of components and services with other new or reused components to form the system solution.

Component suppliers and consumers

> We think globally, specification is in Europe, construction is in India, and assembly is in the USA; Select Perspective supports this completely.
>
> Programme manager, ERP product supplier

All successful economic systems are based on the supplier–consumer model; this supply chain is the engine of economic success (Figure 2.1). We can enjoy that success by applying the same model to delivering software solutions.

Obviously, business solutions are responses to the needs of the business. This is worth restating, because to build solutions without a need is a waste of precious capital and human resources. This solution delivery process is a consumer of components and services. It may construct other software parts, but generally it defines the particular services, such as tax calculations, required for the solution.

The component suppliers have their own delivery process, which responds to requests for services and supplies matching components. It is driven by a need for a particular set of services rather than a business need.

Figure 2.1
Supplier–consumer model

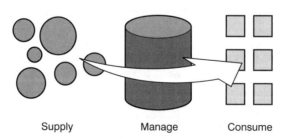

Supply   Manage   Consume

To connect suppliers to consumers there is a person, team, or technology that acts as a broker to the parties. This 'broker' facilitates the flow of requests and responses between the different groups. The implication of this model is that the suppliers and consumers are different organizations, groups, teams, etc. This may be so, but they are in fact different roles that can be fulfilled by people within a small team on their particular project. For larger projects, the roles may be filled by other teams, groups, etc. Select Perspective encourages and supports the community of component suppliers and consumers.

Real-world process

Proven in real-world, small- to large-scale IT efforts, Select Perspective has been refined over several years into a collection of highly practical, tightly focused best practices for solution development. It enables IT organizations to take safe, low-risk steps into CBD for both small- and large-scale projects.

Select Perspective has three enduring principles:

1 *Small set of key deliverables*: e.g. a use case diagram or a class model. If any diagram is not necessary to a particular solution then you do not produce it; anything not on the delivery line has been ruthlessly pruned.

2 *Based on experience*: experience gained by many consultants working over many years with numerous customer teams to deliver successful solutions; team sizes have ranged from a few developers to large globally distributed teams, all with different skill levels.

3 *Designed to fit most organizations* and recognizes that each organization is different. It can therefore be adapted to fit existing processes within an organization, or it can be a new foundation from which to start and then adapt as experience grows.

These principles make Select Perspective fit for real-world solution delivery.

Some methodologies tend to revolve around one technique, such as use case modeling or database design. This is simply too limiting for IT organizations that need to build sophisticated applications. To more fully support design activities, Select Perspective seamlessly integrates the three major kinds of visual modeling technique – business process modeling (BPM), Unified Modeling Language (UML), and data modeling. This allows designers to start anywhere and use the right tool for the right job, producing a better result.

Select Perspective development life cycle

> The iterative life cycle and parallel working not only delivered the project on time, it gave me and the stakeholders confidence in the team at every stage.
>
> Project manager, leading fashion retail organization

The Select Perspective software development life cycle is a set of workflows that are based on an iterative and incremental development approach. Iterations allow projects to meet changing requirements and modify remaining activities and deliverables as necessary. Increments deliver functioning and tested slices of the solution, which are treated as project milestones.

In practice, increments are determined from the priorities of the business and/or the removal of any perceived technical risk such as a new middleware platform. Iterations occur both within and between increments. During an increment there will be a number of iterations of deliverables such as component specifications, and screen layouts. Further activities in the increment are then adjusted if necessary. Between increments, there is a re-evaluation of the business and technical priorities.

Consume workflow

We were very clear on our roles and what to specify for the developers.

Business analyst, major insurance organization

The consume workflow (Figure 2.2) delivers the solution then maintains and supports that solution. This workflow contains five major workflows, with two administrative workflows for planning and support.

Activities in business alignment, business architecture, and solution delivery are such that these workflows can start at the same time. For example, business alignment captures the business requirements, which may require the development of some prototype screens to aid user understanding; prototyping user screens is part of solution delivery.

Business alignment delivers the business process models, the use cases describing the functional requirements, and the user acceptance test scripts. Business architecture delivers the component specifications together with their test specifications. Solution delivery consumes the components from the component suppliers; it adds the user interface components and then merges with

Figure 2.2
Consume workflow

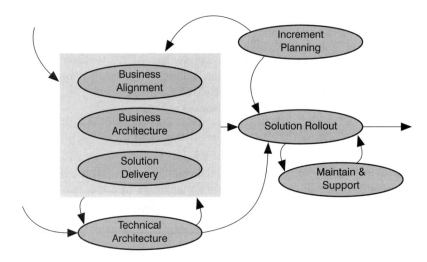

the technical architecture components to deliver the solution. This solution may or may not be rolled out depending on the delivered functionality, e.g. incremental delivery.

Key to this parallel working is increment planning. This determines which activities within these workflows are to be undertaken for each new increment. Essential, but often forgotten until the last minute, is the technical architecture. The technical architecture workflow delivers base and facility components for the target solution platform, which are merged via Select Perspective Patterns™ with the business components to provide a reliable framework for the solution.

Supply workflow

> Even though we are remote from the business users, the component specifications made it so easy.
>
> Systems developer, major insurance organization

The supply workflow (Figure 2.3) delivers and maintains components. When a request for services is received there is a negotiation on the specification. For example, this may involve splitting some services, or supplying two components, or even altering the service specification to take advantage of existing components. This results in an agreed component specification, which is a form of contract between the component developers and their consumers.

The component is designed, constructed, and fully tested before being delivered to the consumers. Subsequent change requests cause the normal impact analysis, updates, and regression testing activities to be performed before the update is issued.

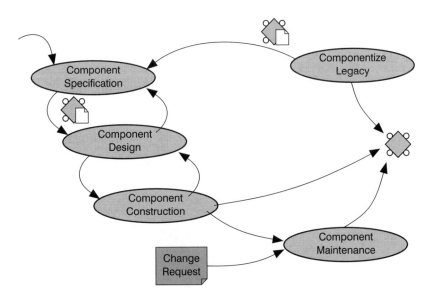

Figure 2.3
Supply Workflow

So far, this workflow description has been about new components, but components can also be extracted from existing legacy systems. The supply workflow assesses the componentization strategy – wrapping, re-engineering, reverse engineering – and tackles the changes, hopefully without disrupting the operational system. Some areas of the legacy system will no longer be suitable, so component specifications, derived from the existing code, need to be drafted and used to construct new components. This typically happens when the existing functionality lacks the performance for a new solution. Select Perspective integrates legacy harvesting into CBD.

Component management workflow

In the component management workflow (Figure 2.4), there are two distinct streams. One stream is concerned with the acquisition, certification, and publication of components and services. The other stream centers on locating and retrieving candidate components for reuse.

Components and services can be acquired from a number of sources. First, there has to be a definition of the acquisition strategy, e.g. business components to be built, all others to be bought. Based on this strategy, component specifications can be accumulated and issued to the organization's development teams, or to trusted partners, or sought from commercial sources.

When the candidate component arrives it undergoes formal testing and certification, which means that it can be rejected. If the component is certified, then after classification and storage in a component repository it is published for access by potential reusers.

Figure 2.4
Manage Workflow

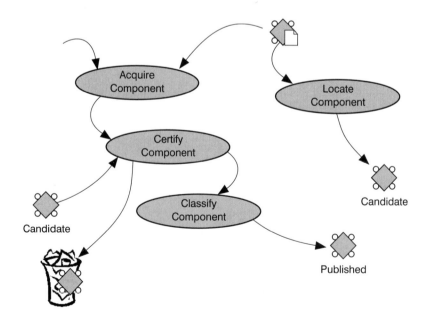

When solution or component developers have specified the services required for their construction work, they then search the component repository for suitable components and services. Whenever components are discovered they can be retrieved and examined, perhaps even tested, before they are reused. Select Perspective supports all forms of component and service acquisition.

Project types

A danger with most process descriptions is that they fit only one kind of project, most commonly a *greenfield* (empty field on which to build something) development. Select Perspective caters for this kind of project, but it recognizes that there are different kinds of project that demand adjustments to the process workflows:

- *Brownfield* development projects are treated as part of the normal (greenfield) process on the assumption that there will be legacy systems.
- *Web-driven* development has extra activities associated with the web content delivery, technical architecture and the deployment of the solution, e.g. to 'web farms'.
- *Legacy rejuvenation* projects need extra care in key areas to ensure a successful rejuvenation.
- *Integrating packaged solutions* into the business and systems environments involves changes to the basic process.

Different types of project appear at regular intervals, usually driven by some new technology such as mobile agents. Select Perspective is able to adapt to these new project types.

Agile software development

Throughout the history of software development, there has been an ongoing debate between the advocates of formalized structured methodologies such as the 'V' life cycle and SSADM, and the proponents of iterative, prototype-based approaches such as Rapid Application Development (RAD) and Boehm's Spiral Method. Time and again, the debate between formal methodologies and simpler approaches has reached the same conclusion: *that elements of both are needed to meet the requirements of the superset of all projects*. It is only by considering the specific needs of a project at its inception that a decision on the development approach can be made.

Once again, the same debate is raging anew. This time the enemy is complexity, espoused by heavyweight methodologies such as the Rational Unified Process (RUP). The rebels fly the banner of eXtreme Programming, (XP), turning their backs on complex development and modeling approaches by returning to the roots of development: the programming code.

However, XP proponents reluctantly admit the need for some kind of core approach, aimed once again at a balance between the fast-moving requirements of development teams and the longer-term needs of the enterprise. There is recognition that any processes, methods, and tools need to be flexible not just at the start of a project but throughout its length as new needs arise and new risks have to be mitigated. These are the key elements of facilities for what is termed *agile software development*.[1] As Select Perspective is agile, it can flex to become more extreme-like, or even rigorous at the RUP end. This said, Select Perspective could not be bent into an RUP-style waterfall.

Agile software development requires *agile processes*, and one thing these processes can never be is an 'off-the-shelf' methodology. Any textbook methodology that expresses sequencing of activities inevitably constrains the execution of those activities. If it is large, it will appear monolithic; if small, it will be inadequate for the more complex of needs. In reality, we can make things even simpler by stating: 'a defined process can neither be agile nor inflexible; it is how it is applied that counts'.

If Select Perspective is delivered only as a hard-copy manual, although inherently agile, then it could not be considered a truly agile process. It includes a multitude of activities that may be applied to every conceivable software development situation. It also incorporates best practice principles, which may be applied by team members and project managers alike. To be agile, Select Perspective requires mechanisms to enable the process to react to changing circumstances. Process management tools, such as Select Process Director, provide these mechanisms. These tools enable managers and planners to:

- Define the most appropriate process for the project in hand, often providing a number of process patterns, for example for simpler 'greenfield' projects, for legacy integration, or for web application development.

- Customize the process to meet the needs of the project. In any process, some activities are optional and may be included or excluded. Other processes have alternatives, for example to cope with greater or lesser complexity, while others are required but have already been carried out and do not have to be repeated. The tool will guide the manager through the process, enabling informed decisions on what to include, exclude, or replace.

- Assess the risks and make adjustments to the process at any stage. Potential risks are presented to the project manager together with explanations and mitigations. The latter may include recommendations to include or exclude activities from the process.

- Incorporate actual project data. Synchronization with project plans enables initial plans to be generated and resourced, saving time to be spent on real project issues rather than administration.

Proponents of extreme agile development are often opposed to the use of design techniques, in particular modeling of requirements or design features prior to

1. Also sometimes called *adaptive software development*.

coding. For example, use cases have been criticized as a key cause of 'analysis paralysis' in which the models become a drain on development resources, reducing the time available to develop the application. From its inception Select Perspective has advocated the use of multiple, best-of-breed modeling techniques[2] both text- and diagram-based. These techniques exist as a kit bag that simplifies the lives of business analysts and developers alike. Select Perspective does not advocate the use of all the techniques, all the time; only the essential models need to be used to understand an application and its context.

Summary

Select Perspective is invaluable for CIOs, IT directors, project managers, analysts and solution designers and developers who need a contemporary software development process that meets the many demands of modern solution delivery. Select Perspective is a comprehensive development life cycle for component-based solutions that supports business-aligned parallel development in order to reduce time-to-market.

2. For example, Select Perspective was the first to link Ivar Jacobsen's use cases with Grady Booch's class models.

Supply 3

Supply is about the provisioning of components and services, whether these are reused, rented, bought, or built. This chapter outlines the different ways in which components and services can be supplied and gives more detail[1] on the activities for designing and constructing components. It is not a prescriptive process. Instead, the process may be customized to meet the needs of the project: some activities are optional and may be included or excluded; others have alternatives, while others are required but have already been carried out and do not have to be repeated.

The normal approach to supplying components is to build them, and this is covered in detail in the later component delivery workflow. With the rise of web services, however, other options to building are now available, e.g. renting a service. From a straightforward development point of view, there is little difference between using a component and a web service; each is a black box that provides a certain type of functionality exposed through one or more interfaces.

Regardless of whether the functionality will be implemented as a component or a service, certain choices about how to obtain the required functionality must be made:

- reuse existing functionality that is available within your organization;
- rent the functionality from an external source;
- buy the functionality in from an external source;
- build your own functionality.

This gives a common development principle or mantra: *'reuse before rent, before buy, before build'*.

Table 3.1 compares the difference choices with components or with the use of web services.

1. Full details can be found in the Select Process Director version of Select Perspective.

Table 3.1   Build versus buy for components and services

	Components	Web services
Build	Create components to house some or all of application functionality. These components may or may not form part of a reuse strategy.	Create services to house some or all of application functionality. For most applications, this will be very similar to performing a decomposition of the required functionality into components. The creation of a web service to embody application functionality should be considered carefully. If there is no intention for the functionality to be used outside the application (at the current time), then it may be better to stick with the creation of static components.
Reuse	Existing components developed, harvested, or bought in are available in the organizational component library. These are extracted, licensed and used to deliver some of the application functionality.	Existing web services developed, harvested, or bought in are available through the organizational web service registry. This registry may be accessed through a web service librarian or dynamically through a UDDI registry. Web services are discovered and used to deliver some of the application functionality. The application developer must ensure that the service meets appropriate levels of systemic quality for availability, scalability, etc. This may involve negotiation and agreement with the providers of the service or an organizational team of web service librarians/suppliers. The web service interface information is then imported into the application.
Rent	Not really applicable – see **Buy**.	Third-party web services are identified that can deliver some of the application functionality. An agreement is reached with the third party on cost and levels of systemic quality. The web service interface information is then imported into the application. These services may already form part of the organizational web service registry.
Buy	Third-party components are identified and bought in to deliver some of the application functionality. These components may already form part of the organizational component library.	Not really applicable – see **Rent** – unless the organization buys the rights to deploy and host the web service and its dependent implementation on their own web/application servers.

Making the supply decisions

Supply decisions can be made once you have defined your units of functionality then identified and allocated these to an architectural layer.[2] These decisions consider whether each functional unit should be a component or a web service and whether they can be reused/rented/bought/built (R/R/B/B). For most applications, the considerations in Table 3.2 hold true.

The central issue in the use of services as opposed to components is that of *provenance*. In addition to its functionality, certain quality and cost judgments must be made about a service that are not necessarily required for a component. For example:

- Will the service provider or the specific service still be here next year, i.e. for the anticipated lifetime of the application? This is much more important in terms of rented services than it is for bought components. Should a component provider go out of business, the component will not stop working. However, it is quite a different matter to run a service yourself.

- What is the cost model of the service? There may be a purchase or licensing cost, as there would be for a component. Many services will charge a per-transaction cost as well as or instead of an up-front charge. There may be a significant cost associated with the development and testing of the service if a service charges per transaction.

- Use of a service may increase the cost of the application over the life cycle. Any subscription-based service will need the subscription renewing every year as well as an ongoing service or per-transaction charge.

- Does the service provide the appropriate level of systemic quality? In some cases such as availability, the required level can be gained through the use of multiple services.[3] Other qualities such as security, require a minimum level since a breach in security of the service may lead to a breach of the application security as a whole.

- If the service is accessed across the public internet, what impact will this have in terms of scalability and availability? All parts of the path between your organization and the target web service must be assessed for the impact of traffic peaks and service outages. For example, what sort of bandwidth and availability can your internet service provider (ISP) guarantee for your internet connection?

2. Briefly, these architectural layers consist of:
   - low-level infrastructure, including the hardware, operating systems, and virtual platforms such as Enterprise Java and .NET;
   - web services applied as part of the technical infrastructure; examples include authentication, long-running transactions, and management;
   - web services applied at the business level; examples range from relatively fine-grained services such as currency conversion and payment processing, through to coarser-grained services such as credit checks and hosted ERP functionality;
   - the application's business logic;
   - the application's user interface.
   Components identified within the application reside in one of these layers.
3. You could gain 99.99% availability through having a certain number of 99.9% availability services you can use at any one time.

Table 3.2 Choosing components or services and how to get them

Layer	R/R/B/B decision	Rationale
Low-level infrastructure	Buy	Low-level infrastructure, as defined previously in the application architecture, is very much a commodity. It will be bought in as a component (hardware, operating system, and virtual platform) and installed. Although this could be delegated to an ASP, essentially this level consists of bought-in components (not web services).
Infrastructure web services	Rent or Buy	Web services at the infrastructure level will often be bought in the same way that components at the same functional level will be bought. For some web services, this may actually involve buying in the software and hosting it as an internal web service. Frequently, however, the web service will be rented from a third party and accessed remotely. This level of web service will rarely be built in-house, hence there is also very low possibility for reuse. However, such services may be built in-house during the initial days of third-party web service provision.
Business web services	Build, Reuse, Rent or Buy	Web services at the business level are subject to many of the same considerations as those at the infrastructure level. Depending on the application, there may be specific requirements for business-level web services that are not addressed by third parties. However, these services may not be unique to the business logic for the specific application being built; an example may be actuarial calculations in an insurance firm. In this case, a web service may be built and operated for this application, with the possibility of subsequent reuse in later applications.
Business logic	Build or Reuse	The business logic is such an integral part of the application that it will not be bought or rented from a third party. Business logic available inside the organization may be reused if appropriate. This may take the form of either components or web services.
User interface	Build or Buy	The user interface is such an integral part of the application that it will not be bought or rented from a third party. Since the user interface defines the precise intent of the application, it will not usually be possible to reuse existing components or web services.

Component delivery

The main development process on the supply side of the supply–manage–consume approach to component-based development is *component delivery*. These activities define the component services, specify the internal architecture in terms of its classes, and combine with the technical infrastructure to deliver an executable package for the component. This is a view of the component based on concepts that are meaningful to analysts, developers, and programmers.

Component delivery is a generic workflow that covers the different types of component: business, technical, and data. Each type of component has the same set of activities within the workflow, but each will have its own specialist developers, techniques, and mindset that deliver the component model, and the executable.

Although the workflow shown in Figure 3.1 has the appearance of a typical waterfall process of specify–design–construct–maintain, this hides the fact that the prioritization of component services drives each pass through these stages. Service priorities are set by the *solution team*, which in turn follows the use case priorities set by the business stakeholders. For example, the first set of use cases may require only two or three services from the component rather than the full set, so the subsequent design and development focuses on these few services. Iteration happens with each subsequent set of use cases. However, some delivery teams may not apply such an iterative approach and may choose to undertake a thorough specification and design of the component, then prioritize the construction according to the demands of the use cases.

Figure 3.1
Component delivery
workflow

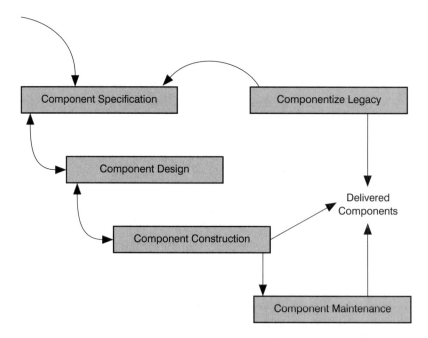

Basic workflow

The first step is to define and agree the *component specification* with the possible consumers of the component. This means examining the requirements shown in the various architecture models – business, technical, and data – and then specifying the requirements of the component in terms of its responsibilities and services.

Once the services have been agreed, the next step is to design the internal architecture of the component in terms of its classes. These parts of the component can be then constructed and combined with the technical infrastructure to deliver the set of agreed and prioritized services. When this has been successful, the component executable is built for the target environment(s), and finally the component is tested to ensure that its functional and non-functional requirements are satisfied; this is often done by a separate test team.

When dealing with the supply of components, it is necessary to consider maximizing the investment in existing applications by reusing the contained functionality as a set of services for new applications, i.e. componentization of legacy systems. In providing these services, various levels of effort and approach are required to integrate the application: wrapping legacy application functionality; re-engineering the legacy application; and/or reverse engineering the functionality (see later section).

After the component has been delivered it then enters the maintenance and support phase, which ensures that it continues to meet the needs of its users. Component maintainers respond to reports of failures, and requests for changes or enhancements, then after evaluation they allocate change requests to item owners for resolution.

Define component specification

Defining and agreeing the specification of the component's services is a key step in delivering successful solutions. The resulting component specification is a *contract* between the supplier and consumers that has been negotiated between all parties. This specification guides both the design and construction of the internals, as well as providing an interface that other solution developers can use.

An agreed component specification includes:

- details of the service interfaces, including each service signature;
- the environment in which the component is going to be used and deployed; and
- a black-box test specification, which is used to determine whether the delivered component meets the requirements defined in the component specification.

To help to achieve agreement on the specification, a component management tool (see Chapter 11) is used to publish each iteration so that comments and feedback from the component's user community can be reviewed and any issues arising resolved.

Design component

This step in component delivery provides a model of the *internal architecture* of the component in terms of its classes, defines the data services required, and may produce or update the persistent data model. UML analysis techniques are used to model the component's internal structure to deliver the required component services; an example is shown in Figure 3.2. This means identifying candidate classes and their attributes, assigning class responsibilities, and identifying class relationships. During all stages, it is recommended that any design decisions be documented. Finally, the component's object model is reviewed by others in the component delivery team.

Once the classes have been agreed, the next step is to identify their behavior (class methods). This involves producing object interaction diagrams (see Figure 3.3 for an example) for each component service and, perhaps, state diagrams for key classes. As each class will have data requirements, it is important at this point to identify the services required from data components. Data components are used to separate the database technology from the business components. Similarly, it may be necessary to define the component's *persistent data model*.[4]

As usual, the final step is to evaluate the component design by reviewing the object model and persistent data model to determine whether they are fit for their purpose and meet defined quality standards.

Construct component

Constructing the component involves realizing the design of the component combined with the technical infrastructure to deliver a tested set of services. As stated earlier, scheduling the parts in the component that are to be constructed is determined by the use case priority, i.e. 'build only what you need now'. So, for each component, service to be implemented, only those operations on classes involved in delivering the service need be constructed. This may be a very small part of the overall component, so we are not spending time on unnecessary items.

This activity has slight differences in the early steps for each type of component:

- *business components* require data and technical components to realize the solution. The business object model is elaborated to show these data and technical services, including the application of technical architecture patterns. These applied patterns incorporate the technical infrastructure, components and services defined by the technical architecture team;
- *data components* deliver a set of services for the given data component specification. They may also use technical architecture patterns such as transaction management in their construction;

---

4. The organization of data into records or tables according to DBMS architectural constraints but independently of physical characteristics.

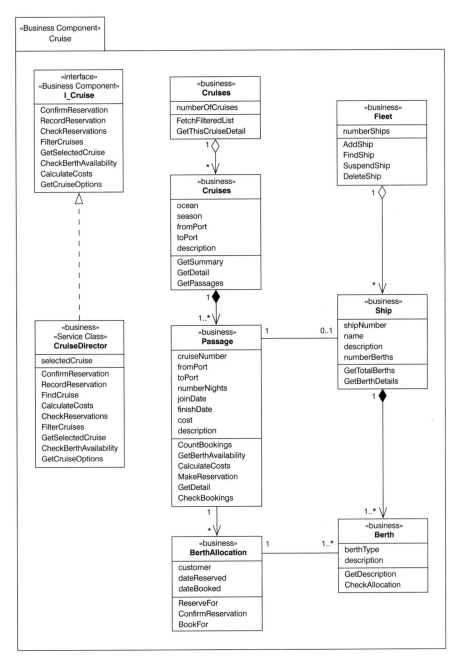

Figure 3.2
Example of an
internal component
class diagram

Figure 3.3
Example of an component internal interaction diagram

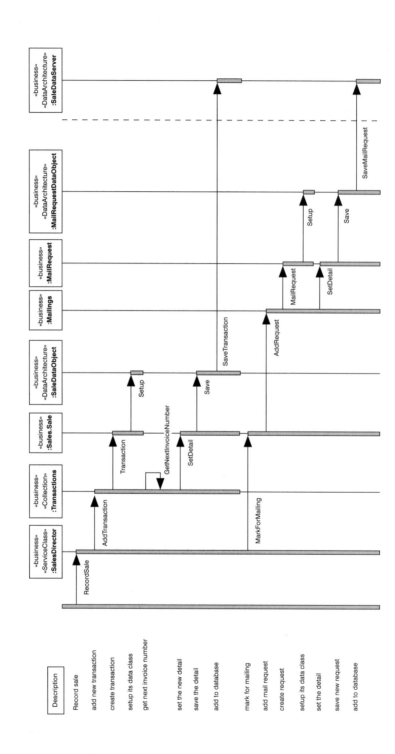

- *technical components* such as base classes and facility components such as an error handler may require data component services and their own base classes.

A simple example of the interrelationships between the different types of component is shown in Figure 3.4.

The example shows a business class as a subclass of a base class delivered by the technical architecture team, and it uses a technical component and facility class supplied by the same technical team. Part of the business class is its data class, which marshals information between the class and a data component,

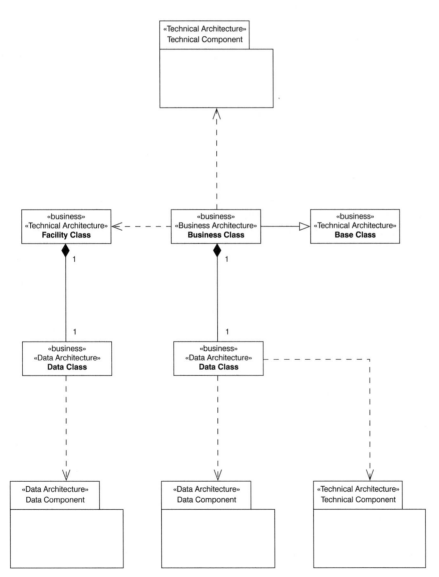

Figure 3. 4
Example of the inter-relationships between the different types of component

which handles the database operations. This data class may also use the services of a technical component such as the error handler. The class/data class/data component pattern is also repeated for the facility class.

The major activity is the actual construction of the component: writing the code to support the component object design for the given service. Many UML tools, including Select Component Factory, automatically generate code for the classes, attributes, and methods, but it is left to the developer to code the logic for each method. During the task of translating the models into physical code, the developer must apply some thought and add missing detail. Any temptation to change the design without consulting the designer must be avoided.[5]

During construction, frequent unit testing establishes whether the code for a given component service works correctly, and if it does not, to identify where it has gone wrong. Unit testing is informal and is performed by the developer who wrote the code. It gives the developer confidence that the code is functioning correctly before it is handed over for formal testing.

Before the component can be released, the developer should document both the build environment, and the component containership of runtime facilities, e.g. error handling, transaction control, the deployment of the component, and its dependencies on other components.

Test and rollout component

Now that the component has been released by the development team, it is time for the test team to determine whether the component executable/package satisfies the component's functional and non-functional requirements. This involves executing a series of tests and evaluating the results of these tests.

Execute tests means running test scripts defined for this increment as well as running those scripts for previous increments to ensure that the latest changes have not broken existing services (i.e. regression testing). All tests need to be performed under black-box conditions to verify the external behavior of the component. If the tests fail, then the component developer must identify and fix the problem; it is not the test team's responsibility to fix the component, as there may be errors in the OO analysis, the design or the code. All test results – good and bad – are documented. When the tests are passed, then rollout means publication of the tested component executable/package to the component user community.

Componentization of legacy systems

In order to maximize the investment in current applications, it may be necessary to use the existing functionality by providing a set of services for new applications. In providing these services, various levels of effort and approach are required to integrate the application. These efforts can deliver *wrapper components*, which:

5. Some component development tools allow synchronization of the code with the (earlier) models.

- encapsulate unchanged functionality in the legacy application;
- component specifications containing the functional requirements extracted for the existing legacy application through reverse engineering; and
- components that encapsulate the re-engineered functionality extracted from the legacy application.

The initial step is to define the *integration strategy* by assessing the application architecture. This assessment is to understand the legacy application so well that any candidate component packets of functionality can be determined. Then the technical options are assessed to determine the feasibility of different componentization strategies based on the current technical environment of the application. When these option assessments have been completed, they must be agreed to ensure the feasibility of an appropriate componentization strategy, as more than one approach can be applied in any situation: wrapping, re-engineering, and reverse engineering.

Wrapping

A wrapper is a component that provides a message-based interface to non-object-oriented software such as the functionality within a legacy application. To provide a wrapper, first analyze the legacy application by examining the available documentation to give a focus to your efforts, e.g. there will be parts that do not lend themselves to wrapping. Then if the code is available (for package integration this may not be the case) analyze the legacy code for distinct functional parts. All details of chosen function and their data as well as identified constraints or non-functional issues must be recorded. This technique can be called 'legacy archaeology'.[6]

Once a candidate wrapper component has been identified, draft the initial service specification to include methods, signatures, and events (e.g. exceptions, preconditions, and post-conditions for each service); model the wrapper component interface; apply design patterns; and design the internal classes that handle the mapping of services to functions (wire-through). New classes that enhance or extend the existing functionality, e.g. performing extra validations, can also be included.[7] The last few steps mean creating the test cases, reviewing and agreeing the design specification, and publishing the agreed wrapper component specification. Now build and test the wrappers like any other component.

Re-engineering

Re-engineering the legacy application means altering the existing functionality or interfaces to meet the new business needs. This would be performed under processes and activities agreed for that type of application, e.g. mainframe procedures.

6. Undertaking 'mining' of the code and documentation to harvest suitable functionality.
7. These wrappers are called *adapters*, as they adapt the functionality of the legacy system.

Reverse engineering

Reverse engineering means using the existing logic and data descriptions as specifications for new components, i.e. recreating the same functionality within a new environment. This involves analyzing the source code for candidate components, clustering data items into logical groups to determine the potential of such candidates, clustering functions to match data items, then detecting the responsibilities of the new component. Once that has been done, it is possible to generalize the services and publish the component specification. This specification becomes an input to the component delivery process.

Whichever approach is taken, you must be aware of the risks involved in integrating new and old systems:

- changes to legacy code may impact the wrapper component;
- the required functionality may be inaccessible;
- the level of complexity and dependencies may be too high;
- changes to the legacy application may affect the new system;
- legacy code may be too hard to understand;
- there may be no sources of expertise in the legacy application.

These risks must not be taken too lightly, as they have often been a significant cause of project failure.

Maintain component

Like all software artifacts, a component cannot be ignored once delivered. The team must always ensure that a delivered component continues to meet the needs of its users by responding to reports of failures (defects) and requests for changes or enhancements.

To resolve a defect first update the *defect log*, then recreate the incident and determine a candidate solution. An agreed solution is used to update the component specification and issue it to the component delivery team.

To resolve change requests first identify the affected items, and determine the impact and feasibility of change before scheduling the change. Changes may be categorized in many ways, although the most common is:

- *important and urgent*: schedule as soon as possible;
- *important and non-urgent*: schedule as resources allow;
- *not important but urgent*: schedule as soon as practical;
- *not important and non-urgent*: schedule if possible.

Whenever changes are planned, it is useful to update the *risk register* to reflect the increased risk of doing the change (ripple effect) and for not doing the change (reduced functionality). The updated component specification is then issued ready for the start of the scheduled component delivery process to incorporate the changes.

Technical architecture

Components must guarantee that they can 'inter-operate', i.e. coexisting and cooperating within a common technical environment. Therefore, supplying a technical architecture is key to the successful delivery of component- or service-based solutions.

Delivery of the technical architecture is achieved in two stages. In the first stage, the initial technical architecture is assembled and delivered. This is just like the execution of a normal CBD project, except that a *technical solution* is delivered rather than a business solution. This is known as the *technical architecture delivery*.

In the second stage, the technical architecture is applied to multiple development projects. As each project is executed, the technical architecture is assessed in terms of its fitness for purpose, gaps that must be filled, and novel technical issues introduced by the project. Over time, the technical architecture is extended and refined to meet the changing technical challenges presented by the many development teams. This is called *technical architecture integration*.

Full details of how these are achieved are covered in the section 'Technical architecture' in Chapter 5.

Summary

Supply is about the provision of components and services, whether these are reused, rented, bought, or built. Whichever way they are provided, specification and modeling are required. Specification ensures that the appropriate services are provided, and modeling ensures that the designers interface with these services in their own designs. If the component or service is built, then the models are more comprehensive as they include the internal design of the component. Executables and packages are then assembled with other components and services to provide solutions. A component management tool is critical to the success of the supply process.

The main deliverables from this process are:

- component or service specification
- component or service model
- component executable
- component package.

Manage 4

Reusing components and services has the potential to solve many of the key issues of contemporary software development: faster time-to-market, reduced development and maintenance costs, faster response to change, and improved quality. An *ad hoc* approach to reuse usually exists within individual projects by developers sharing components, from both a black-box and white-box point of view. White-box reuse is quite common among the developer community, where an identified component piece of code 'almost' serves the purpose of a project need and is subsequently customized. However, moving from an *ad hoc* to a managed approach to reuse is not simply a matter of buying a component management tool (see Chapter 11), and publishing a few components and services, although this is a positive first step.

To fully exploit the benefits and instill a culture of reuse within an organization, the following are crucial:

- *A reuse strategy and approach*: the plan for establishing managed reuse within the organization.

- *A process for managing components*: the activities and roles supporting reuse fit into a classic supply–manage–consume process model. Supply activities are the responsibility of component or service providers, whether they are internal or external to the organization. Certification, publication, and maintenance activities are the responsibility of the component management team. Finding, evaluating, and applying are the responsibility of the consumers.

- *Tools to support the process*: automation of the process is key to ensuring successful adoption, as is integration with other application development tools.

- *Components and services*: stocked catalogs of useful components.

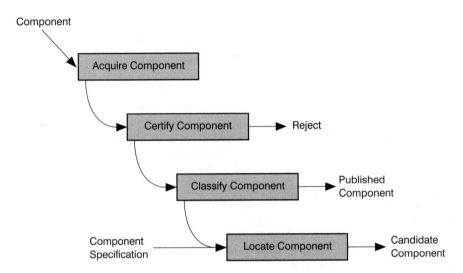

Figure 4.1
Component
management
workflow

Sure-fire ways of quickly losing consumer confidence in a reuse program are:

- *Promoting empty catalogs of components*: if the cupboard is bare, confidence in the initiative will soon be lost.
- *Making it difficult to find and evaluate a component*: even if the repository is stocked, if you can't find what you are looking for confidence will be lost and your components and services become your 'best-kept secret'.
- *Publishing poor-quality components and services*: consumers should be provided with a rich set of information that describes the component. This will help to locate and assess its applicability.
- *Ignoring configuration control*: over the lifetime of components, changes and releases will need to be reflected by versioning.

To insure against such factors, and also to realize the value of reuse, the key activities of acquisition, quality assurance, publication, and maintenance of the component assets are critical.

Component management, shown in Figure 4.1, describes a formalized process framework that, when applied in a corporate environment, enables the supply–manage–consume model.

Acquire component

So what components and services will be useful? Where will they be acquired? The task of identifying business needs that can be fulfilled by components is essential prior to any acquisition; a good starting point for this identification is a review of current and future project needs in terms of:

- common UI aspects across solutions;
- recurring technical architecture themes, such as error handling;
- specific business domains for common business concepts; and
- commonality across business domains.

During this exercise a basic *component classification*, i.e. categorization of component types, is being established, e.g. user interface 'widget', technical, or business-specific such as human resources. To implement this basic classification and aid management and reuse of the emerging components, a *component repository* is structured in terms of catalogs, whose structure reflects this classification of the component.

There may well be many identified types of component and service that meet a business's needs, and many sources to supply them. Prioritization is key to ensuring acquisitions match demand. Priorities are influenced and affected by a whole host of factors, and over time priorities will indeed change. Factors to consider when assessing priorities are:

- Standard architectures are an essential part of CBD: reliance on the availability of common architectural solutions is high. To facilitate compliance with an architecture, it is common to provide for essential services and protocols by way of architecture or infrastructure components.
- Commodity components are widely available. They can be specifically targeted based on current or upcoming projects and represent low-risk, quick-buy decision. Examples could be web utilities such as shopping carts and credit card validation.

The acquisition of components and services may rely on one or more techniques: purchased, contracted, built, or rented as a web service. There is a growing commercial marketplace for the purchase of components; the marketplace typically caters for commodity components, such as user interface or utilities. If using a web service, it is also necessary to understand the required levels of systemic quality for the service so that these can be documented and agreed in advance with the service provider. For example, the scalability characteristics of the application may be dependent on the scalability of the provided service.

In-house development can organically grow the component assets, or project's build, or procure components and services as they are needed. Early identification of required components, e.g., rejuvenation of legacy systems for integration into the component world, may spawn specific component development initiatives to design and build such components. The separation of component specification from implementation lends itself favorably to a managed mechanism for contracting out the component build, this arrangement may be applicable where scarce resources or insufficient skilled resources constrain the build process.

Establishing *service-level agreements* with suppliers is critical for ongoing maintenance of the component repository. The service levels are very much dependent on the type of supplier and the associated risk. For example, a component supplied in-house with source code represents less risk than an externally supplied component with no source code agreement. Service levels should also enable policy definition regarding the responsibility for maintaining the component. If a component is supplied in binary form (black-box reuse), then maintenance lies with the supplier. When a component is supplied in source form (white-box reuse), either by an outsourced contract or internally constructed, then maintenance usually lies with the supplier. The danger with source code availability is that reusers may affect the code themselves, leading to project-specific clones of components. This underlines the need for service levels and the appropriate policies to be put in place.

Classify and certify component or service

To encourage and enable the reuse of component or service, it must be easy to find it, evaluate what it does and obtain a measure of how well it does it. The basis for this is providing the right information via a rich *classification scheme*, which gathers the relevant information that describes the component or service. The classification scheme must be uniform and therefore applicable to all types of component and service. The scheme should include the following:

- *functionality*: what the component responsibilities are; the specification of the services that the component interface provides;
- *technology*: component standards and platform, e.g. .NET, Enterprise Java;
- *distribution*: distribution and deployment of the component; if the component functionality is provided via web services, then it would also include the web service registration information;
- *commerce*: licensing agreements, support contracts;
- *completeness*: complies with quality characteristics.

The classification scheme can be extended further by introducing meta-information such as keywords and attributes. This provides a richness by which consumers can search the component repository further.

As well as a classification scheme, a *certification scheme* is used to address the quality characteristics of the component. The scheme adopted will depend on a number of factors, such as the level of effort that can be applied to check quality. Any scheme must be responsive to change based on feedback from the consumer community. One simple scheme is based on a measure of how often the component has been used. However, the more formal scheme suggested below requires considerably more effort to apply:

- *Level 1*: no testing, no documentation, unknown level of completeness. This may be acceptable to a project team that urgently requires the component and accepts that it has not been through the full certification process.
- *Level 2*: verified level of completeness, i.e. all deliverables, specification, documentation, test cases, and data are present.

- *Level 3*: test cases and test suites provided and executed; this may also include designing further tests if necessary.
- *Level 4*: fully tested, documented, meets agreed quality criteria – a certified component.

Applying the appropriate levels of classification and certification to the acquired components and services means that they can be published in the component catalog and the component itself stored in the component repository. Publication communicates the availability of reusable components to the developer community. Communication may be in different forms: component catalog, notifications, seminars, newsletters, or bulletin boards. Reuse specialists can also be allocated to projects to communicate their knowledge of reusable components to the project team members.

Maintain components

Maintaining the component repository is essential and ongoing; these activities ensure the continued commitment to preserving the components' assets over their lifetime. The need is particularly evident when considering the following scenario. A component supplier resubmits a component as a result of a change to the component. The change may have been caused by a defect resolution, enhancement to functionality, technology change, and so on. When the component has already been deployed in one or more solutions, the component's users (consumers) need to be aware of this new release and be able to assess its impact on their own solution.

When components and services are reused extensively throughout the organization, it is crucial that their deployment and their reusers are known. This is where modern component management tools assist by tracking and mapping the various deployments.

Maintenance ensures that not only classification standards are met but also, more importantly, that configuration control policies are in place and adhered to. To achieve this, both the component specification and the actual component need version identification. New versions of components and services can be created and linked to older versions. It will also be necessary to archive unused and older versions of components and services. This concept is similar to that of source code configuration management, but it refers to component specifications and completed components; see Figure 4.2. The component specification exists well before any code is created, and this is one of the reasons why mainstream configuration management systems are currently not suited to component management.

Publication and republication of components requires that consumers (reusers) be notified of the availability of software components. This task may be automated with technologies such as e-mail and web-based catalogs. New components and services will typically be advertised, and e-mails could contain a copy of (or pointer to) the new component.

4 Levels of Component Abstraction

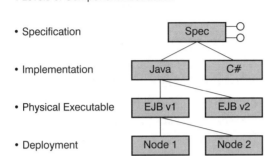

- Specification
- Implementation
- Physical Executable
- Deployment

Figure 4.2
Managing
component parts
and versions

Locate and retrieve candidate component

Component consumers perform this activity: development teams that want to use or reuse components and services. They identify and examine candidate components and services that meet a variety of different search criteria. This may be through the use of a search engine within a component management tool, or through requests to a reuse help desk staffed by reuse experts.

The structure of the component repository (its catalog structure), and the component classification scheme should enable consumers to browse and search for components and services quickly; our components are no longer the best-kept secret.

When a component match is found, it can be considered further for reuse. This may involve evaluating the component to assess its degree of fitness at design time. If a suitable component is not found, then the consumer can publish a *component request* in the form of a required component specification.

Publish a component request

The component librarian receives the component request whose component specification forms the basis of the tendering mechanism to potential suppliers. The librarian has responsibilities for verifying the request, such as the completeness of the specification against the classification scheme. Suppliers are then identified and the request communicated to them. Consumers and suppliers are likely to negotiate the semantics and description of the component. This results in the supplier submitting the agreed component specification for publication, so allowing both suppliers and consumers to work to the same interface. As mentioned earlier, the component specification can be published long before the actual component is delivered.

Monitoring component and service reuse

The ultimate goal of component and service reuse is to achieve a number of benefits for the business:

- to save work through improved productivity and shortened lead times;
- to reduce the number of errors through improved quality;
- to reduce maintenance costs, again by improving productivity; and
- to reduce rework through the thorough requirements analysis imposed by reuse.

But not every software component may be suitable for reuse. Not every component in the libraries is reused. Not every component is worth reusing. And the only way to know is through *measurement*. Measurement serves two purposes: to determine the extent to which defined goals and objectives are being met; and to assess the current situation prior to setting new goals and objectives.

The first steps in setting up the measurement process are to clearly define the metrics, methods of data collection, and how the data are to be analyzed. Consider graphs or pictures as the better way to present the results, because seeing trends and targets gives much more information than raw figures. Also, any measurement process must include verification and validation of data and results, otherwise the figures may be considered suspect.

A suggested set of metrics for monitoring a component or service is:

- *creation costs*: the cost in creating or preparing a component or service for reuse, which may include purchase or rental and reworking;
- *threshold*: the minimum number of times a reusable component or service must be reused to recover its creation costs;
- *usage costs*: measures the costs incurred each time a component or service is reused; includes finding, understanding, modifying and integrating, and any commercial considerations, e.g. rental;
- *target level*: the minimum proportion of a system that is reusable;
- *maintenance costs*: the cost of supporting the component or service (1) for producers and (2) for reusers;
- *commonality*: how frequently the component or service recurs across a set or family of systems.

When measuring the impact of reuse on development, consider productivity, quality and lead time. Productivity is measured as functionality/cost and lead time measured as calendar time/functionality. Cost is measured in person-days, and functionality may be measured in lines of code, components, services or function points. Lines of code are less useful, especially as modern CASE tools generate significant amounts of code. More crucial is the functionality in terms of actual function. For example, a car may measure 15 feet and a bicycle 4 feet (lines of code), but the car has much more functionality than the bike (function points).

Summary

The process for managing components acts as the pivot in the supply–manage–consume model. Component or service supply activities are the responsibility of component suppliers, whether they are internal or external to the organization. Certification, publication and maintenance activities are the responsibility of the component management team. Finding, evaluating and applying are the responsibilities of the component or service consumers.

Component and service management requires a clear reuse strategy and approach, and tools that automate the process such as publication, notification, and tracking of component or service reuse.

The main deliverables from the process are:

- component and service catalog
- component or service specification
- candidate component or service
- certified component or service.

Consume   **5**

Use of components can occur in different contexts: solution delivery consuming business components, or component delivery consuming technical components. The most common context is the delivery of business solutions to fulfill business needs. Only the use and reuse of components makes today's key development objectives consistent with the delivery of solutions that are fully aligned to business needs.

The *consume* process forms an umbrella for all those activities that focus on the project-based delivery of business solutions; see Figure 5.1. The following sections describe each of these major processes in detail. Each project starts by gaining an understanding of requirements and ending with the delivery of one or more business solutions. Within this framework, Select Perspective fully supports the concepts of incremental working and iteration.

As is so frequently pointed out by advocates of XP and Agile Methods, a project is worth nothing unless it succeeds in delivering a working solution. Select Perspective emphasizes the importance of incremental working from the start. Even in very early increments, code can be delivered to operate as a proof of concept and capability. Working incrementally allows project teams to prioritize their delivery activity; high-value requirements can be delivered early, realizing significant business benefit early in the project.

Each workflow in Figure 5.1 is iterative as well as incremental. Iterations enable the project to meet changing requirements, whether in functionality or prioritization. Every iteration starts with the analysis of the current situation and modifies the next set of development activities and priorities accordingly. For example, if entering a new technical domain, then a series of iterations will explore and construct a sound technical architecture during the early stages of the project.

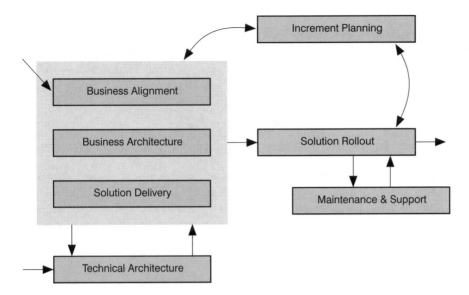

Figure 5.1
Consume process
overview

Iterations also apply to the deliverables from each workflow. Select Perspective focuses on deliverables. Each workflow has a number of deliverables as input and outputs another set of deliverables as products. Hence there is a dependency between workflows based around the flow of deliverables. However, if we wait for a deliverable to be completed, we are back to the waterfall approach to software development. Instead, we accept deliverables in different states (iterations) for each workflow in order that the workflow can start its own activities.

Key to the success of projects is the close alignment of the delivered software with the underlying business needs: an alignment that must be maintained throughout the project, even in the face of a potentially rapidly changing business environment. Incremental working, the continuous involvement of the user community and iteration between and within deliverables are essential characteristics of Select Perspective that help to maintain this close alignment. Not surprisingly, one of the workflows focuses entirely on achieving and maintaining business alignment.

Business alignment

Close alignment between the scope of the intended IT solution and the needs of the business is achieved by providing a formalized view of the *problem domain*. Communication remains the key to this more formal view, so it is still expressed in concepts that are meaningful to the end-user. Based on this view, the boundary of the IT solution is identified and the system requirements are defined. These requirements provide the basis for the user acceptance test plan. A *domain model* can be used to help to justify the project in terms of the benefits provided

Figure 5.2
Business alignment
workflow

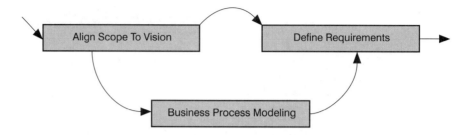

against the costs of implementation. The domain model is made up of a number of different deliverables: business process model, information model, business rules, constraints, etc.

The user community is fully involved throughout the business alignment workflow; see Figure 5.2. Ultimately, the requirements documented during the process are evaluated to ensure they are complete, acceptable and fully meet the business need.

Business process modeling

Consensus between the user community and the development group is key to achieving and maintaining business alignment. Agreement is achieved by modeling the business processes and information that are important within the business area. Ideas are presented using concepts and terminology that are meaningful to the user community. From the developer's viewpoint, the project requirements can be derived from and traceably linked to the domain model, enabling change management as the project proceeds.

Early in the project, the need to create a *business process model* (BPM) is considered. It may not be appropriate, because the intended solution is not focused on process support, for example to include MIS and administrative tools such as directories. The need for agile working and rapid delivery may also reduce the importance of the BPM. However, for process support solutions (i.e. most business IT development projects), a BPM will be an appropriate starting point, especially if process improvement or more radical change is planned.

Business process models consist of two types of diagram: process hierarchy and process threads[1] diagrams. Process hierarchies show the structure of the processes; an example is shown in Figure 5.3. Process thread diagrams show the flow of work through the activities and tasks that make up the process. This will also include manual activities, e.g. 'send brochure'. Figure 5.4 shows an example of a process thread.

There are also two possible kinds of business process model: the 'as-is' and the 'to-be' model. The as-is BPM shows the current activities within the business process as a guide to understanding what happens in the business. However, the to-be BPM, provides the view of the new activities, workflows, etc. that are nec-

1. Also know as activity diagrams.

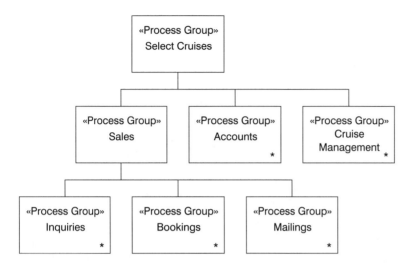

Figure 5.3
Example of a
business process
hierarchy

essary for the planned new process. One common example is the replacement of manual customer services operation by a web-based automated system. Working together, the user community and the development team define and document the issues surrounding current operations. Creation of an as-is BPM often helps to uncover and clarify the issues. The as-is model focuses on the processes impacted by the issues. Issues are usually prioritized by their cost to the business. The 80–20 rule applies very strongly here: 80 percent of the value will be returned by fixing 20 percent of the issues.

Business changes can then be proposed at a high level to resolve the issues on the hit list. A detailed to-be BPM shows how the business changes will be implemented in the organization. Producing the to-be BPM incrementally allows the issues to be tackled in order of priority without waiting for the completion of a potentially long and complex modeling exercise. Furthermore, if acquired components and services are considered to be a possible technical solution, then use of these may open up new possibilities for the business that may impact on the planned business processes.

The result of this activity is a programme of change: business change *and* systems change. Careful planning and coordination are essential in order to ensure that the organization can function during the changes. Basing plans for the delivery of change on the BPM gives a common starting point and ensures that solution deliveries can be synchronized throughout.

Business processes work with information. The value provided by a process is reflected in changes in the information managed by the organization. If the processes are understood, then the information required to operate the processes can also be understood. The *information model* provides a second essential part of the *domain model*. At this stage, the information is understood at a conceptual rather than a physical level, with the definitions becoming more concrete as the project proceeds. Working iteratively with the BPM and information models helps to refine both and to improve the quality of the models.

Figure 5.4
Example of a
business process
thread

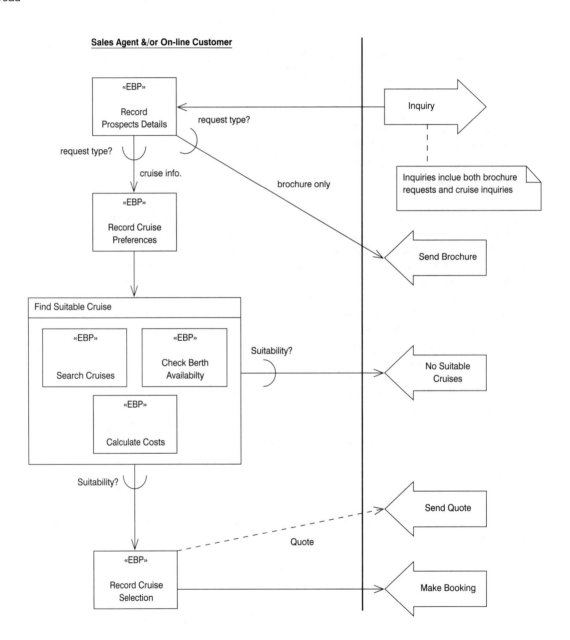

Business processes need decisions to be made. *Business rules* provide the framework for decision making. During the creation of the BPM, information about the important business rules must be recorded. Any business rules are documented at a high level at this stage; further progress with the project will make their definitions more rigorous.

The business processes impose *constraints* on the solutions that will be constructed. Constraints may be in terms of volumes of transactions, response times or failure rates. They may also have a more global impact on the business and technical architectures of the organization. For example, any sales ordering process must have the most up-to-date information on prices and product availability (a constraint), which means that a solution for a out-of-office sales person will require a different architecture to one for an in-office person.[2]

The activities of business process modeling ensure that there is a complete understanding by stakeholders and developers of the actual or planned processes that surround the scope of the project. By producing models of the business processes with their informational needs, rules, and constraints, defining the requirements now becomes straightforward.

Define requirements

Projects often start with a high-level, abstract statement of what is expected by the users. This is not sufficient to act as a full specification of the solutions that must be constructed. From these initial statements, and from other sources such as BPM, more detailed requirements can be derived. However, these derived requirements must be verified with the users in order to ensure that alignment with their initial 'wish list' is maintained. Derived requirements can be categorized as *functional*, describing some aspect of the operation of the system, or *non-functional*, describing some quality that the solutions must display or constraint they must meet.

Services and components may yield new possibilities that should be incorporated into the system requirements. However, care must be taken to consider requirements and not solutions at this stage. There will be some 'givens' in the platform, component and service foundation that impact on the requirements and baseline technical architecture. This provides the landscape within which the solution is specified.

Non-functional requirements

Non-functional requirements describe the quality characteristics that are expected from the delivered solution. They provide a set of metrics to guide the design and

---

2. In this case, the price list and product levels on the remote sales person machine would need to be synchronized on a regular basis, the period depending on the level of change predicted for each of these items, e.g. weekly update for price list, daily update for stock levels.

construction of the solutions and against which they can be tested. Quality characteristics frequently considered include usability, connectivity, availability, integrity, performance, adaptability, security, maintainability, and reliability.

The volumetric information gathered for the BPM is the source for many of the non-functional requirements. The number of times per day that a process is performed is a good indicator of the number of transactions that must be supported. Timing of processes can show how fast the solution must be capable of responding. Such volumetric information also gives a focus for the design, development and testing. For example, if an activity is performed by every user hundreds of times a day, then it will be one of the higher-priority functions. Attention must also be given to ensuring that the user interface does not confuse the user, that the component or service design is optimized, and that there are no system errors through thorough testing.

Criticality of processes imposes constraints on the reliability of the solution. Other non-functional metrics such as usability, maintainability and adaptability are not derived directly from the BPM or other models.

Non-functional requirements will not only drive the design of the solution, they will also be key inputs to the design of the technical architecture that supports the solution. For example, if a web-based solution is required, then the technical architecture must support the delivery of e-systems. If many thousands of 'hits' per hour are expected on the website, then the technical architecture must be capable of supporting this throughput.

Working with the users, the set of key *quality metrics* is selected. Each metric must be measurable, otherwise it will be impossible to agree when the requirement has been fulfilled. Attributes are associated with the metrics. Each attribute has an agreed value that will be tested in the delivered solution. The values are negotiated between the project team and the user community and must be assessed in the light of the business benefit realized. Users may demand 100 percent availability, but if the cost of the solution rises ten fold as a result, then its economic viability will certainly be challenged.

Non-functional requirements do not apply uniformly to the solution as a whole. Overall, the solution may need to be available 98 percent of the time during the working day, five days per week. However, certain key customer support functions may need to be available 99.9 percent of the time, 24 hours per day. The non-functional requirements will form a hierarchy, with broad statements of requirements being decomposed into more detailed, measurable, specific requirements that apply to clearly defined areas of the solution.

Functional requirements

Functional requirements can be seen from different viewpoints. First, there are behavioral requirements for the system: what functionality must be provided for the users, and what will be the solutions' patterns of behavior? If a BPM has been created, these requirements describe how the proposed solution will automate the chosen business processes. Behavioral requirements are documented as *use cases*; each use case describes how business processes will be supported by the business solution. Other use cases may be added to describe the administrative functions required to support the solution itself, rather than the business process: for example, administration of users' access rights to the system. Figure 5.5 shows an example of a use case diagram.

A key difference between the business process and its supporting use case is the scope of description. Business processes must describe all the interactions, including conversations between business actors and the use of documentation

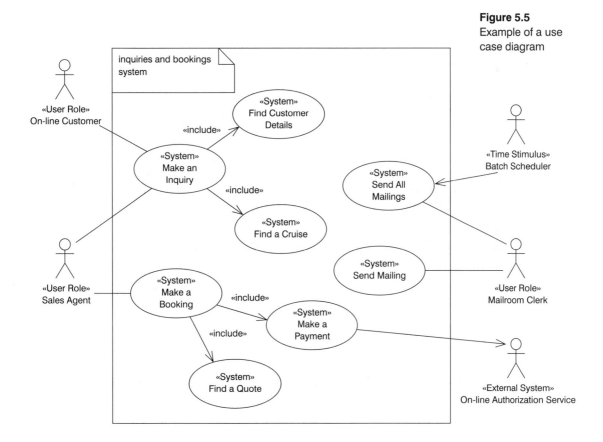

Figure 5.5
Example of a use case diagram

and equipment, only some of which may relate to the proposed business solution. In contrast, the use case focuses only on how the user and system will interact with each other; conversations and use of other artifacts are explicitly excluded from the use case. For example:[3]

1 System present choices of cruises.

2 Actor selects cruise.

3 System presents passages on selected cruise.

4 Actor selects passages.

5 System presents berth details on passage.

6 Actor selects berth(s).

7 System displays costs of cruise.

8 Actor confirms selections.

Use cases are an abstract description of the user interface to the business solution. Prototyping is often used as a more concrete mechanism for agreeing the precise structure, content and layout of the user interface. Working iteratively with the use cases and a user interface prototype[4] helps to ensure the completeness and to refine the content of both views. Having both views of the solution available to the users clarifies the proposed design as it evolves.

A second form of functional requirement is the *business rule*, which expresses rules of procedure and decision making. For example, 'a customer must be more than 18 years of age to obtain a quote'. There are also more complex rules that express algorithms used to calculate results, such as 'the algorithm used to calculate the product discount'. Rules can also be used to express the validation of complex patterns of information.

Business rules are first documented during the creation of the BPM, when their initial statement may be quite high-level, often just a title and brief description. A more complete description is required as part of the functional requirements, so that the complexity of rules and algorithms can be included as a factor in the estimates and plans for the project. In any case, the use cases and prototype will reveal more concrete information about business rules, allowing them to be decomposed into more fine-grained rules and to be specified more completely as the development proceeds.

Use cases are an effective approach to defining functional requirements. These use cases also provide a powerful way to prioritize and plan subsequent development activities (see Chapter 7). In the past, non-functional requirements have been difficult to comprehend and monitor. By using quality metrics that capture the attributes and values, it becomes possible to measure the success or failure of a possible solution.

---

3. Full details are shown in the case study.
4. The user interface prototype is produced as part of the *solution delivery* workflow. if it is to be used to help to confirm the use cases, the project manager should plan the timing of this activity appropriately.

Bringing it all together

Having defined three distinct views of the requirements for the system, in addition to any initial high-level statement of requirements, it is essential that these different facets be unified. Use cases, describing the behavioral requirements for the system, are the hub of the domain model. Every part of the system must be used via its interface. Whether these functions are invoked by users, by other systems, or by timed events, use cases describe the entire external behavior of the system. In other words, every non-functional requirement and every business rule must relate to one or more use cases.

Forming these relationships again helps to verify and refine the different views of the domain model. Are there business rules that do not relate to a use case? Perhaps a use case has been omitted or the business rules are really out of scope. Is there a non-functional requirement that sensibly describes the availability of a given use case? If not, then some key non-functional requirements may have been omitted from the analysis. Integration and cross-verification helps to ensure that the requirements model is of a high quality and retains its close alignment to the initial needs stated by the users and identified in the BPM.[5]

Define acceptance test

This activity defines the external *test cases* for a given aspect of the system. These test cases are used to determine whether a specific deliverable (for example, increment, or solution) meets the requirements defined for it. Multiple test specifications are used as input to the *test plan* for a delivery.

The test specification is defined and developed in parallel with the aspect of the system that it is designed to test. It should become comprehensive by the time the use case, component or service is complete.

The steps involved are:

1 *Review test strategy* to ensure that the test strategy, as currently defined, meets the overall needs of the project.

2 *Refine test approach* to define or refine the approach to testing, given the priorities assigned to the services and the non-functional constraints being applied.

3 *Refine testing requirements*, which document test setup procedures and locations of test data.

4 *Define test environment* suitable for testing the aspects of the system that are being specified. The test environment should be recoverable to its original state for accurate, repeatable testing. This also involves identifying testing tools and the means of testing (e.g. use of a test harness).

5 *Prepare test cases* that evaluate the quality and suitability of the scope element being tested. Test cases contain activities to verify the particular element of the system to be tested. They can be combined into a *test suite*, which runs all tests of a specified type.

5. In contemporary software development, requirements descriptions are no substitute for continuous user involvement.

Justify the project

At any stage[6] of the alignment process the terms of reference, requirements, scope, identified benefits, and potential costs of the proposed project are examined in order to reach a decision on starting the project. This enables the following to be addressed:

- *Risk*: only risks that lie within the cope of the project need be considered and mitigated.
- *Planning*: the scope enables timescales to be calculated and tracked.
- *Decision making*: options and alternatives within the scope can be evaluated.
- *Value*: the costs and benefits of the project can be determined.

During this analysis, the business case for the project will require that any build/buy/rent decision for web services be taken into account. This should include a value assessment of the costs and benefits of using those services over the whole application life cycle, for example to avoid crippling ongoing service licensing costs.

Summary

Business alignment ensures that the requirements of the solution are fully defined. At the hub of these requirements is a use case model supported by the other deliverables in the domain model. The main deliverables from this workflow are:

- domain models
    - business process model
    - use case model
    - business rules catalog
    - non-functional requirements
    - definition of constraints
- user acceptance test plan.

Business architecture

Having identified the requirements for the solution, the first step is to specify the architecture of the application in terms of its *business components*, some of which may be acquired from the component repository. Business architecture is a conceptual view of the solution, based on concepts that are meaningful to the analysts, designers, and developers.

---

6. Usually this occurs after the BPM and use case have been done, but it is recommended as a continuous activity throughout the alignment process.

From the BPM, domain and requirement models it is possible to abstract a view of the overall business architecture supporting the business solution. Three distinct views – process, responsibility, and information – can be analyzed in the existing models and integrated to form a set of candidate components and the dependencies between them. This derived architecture is a starting point. Its contents are expressed in abstract terms and will be altered, re-factored, and refined as design of the solutions proceeds. The main objective is to provide a reasonably stable basis from which to begin.

Business components are the crucial element of the architecture. Once they have been identified in terms of their name, purpose, and main responsibilities, the first attempt at finding a suitable component or service can be made. These components or services are then reused from the component repository. Reuse may introduce constraints, which in turn may require further refinement of the business architecture.

Having produced an initial specification of the required components, the services provided by each component can be analyzed. This may lead to further revisions of the business architecture. *Business services* are fully documented to provide a detailed definition of the interface of each component. Further attempts at finding components or services in the component repository can be made; again the business architecture may be re-factored as a result. Figure 5.6 shows the two major activities of the business architecture workflow.

Implementation of new or altered components is requested by the publication of their specifications in the component repository. At this point, control of the delivery of the component services passes from the consume side to the supply side of the supply–manage–consume cycle. The final design and implementation of the component will be the result of negotiations between the suppliers (internal or external) and the (various) consumers.

Identify business components

Significant amounts of information about the business solutions have already been gathered in the form of requirements, including BPM and use cases. All these sources of information are used to help to derive the architecture of candidate business components; see Figure 5.7. Three facets of thinking help with the derivation of candidate components: business process, responsibilities, and information.

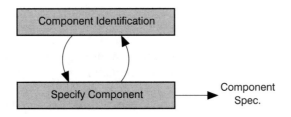

Figure 5.6
Business
architecture workflow

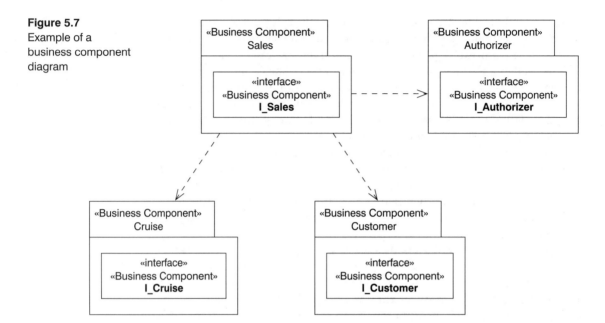

Business process

Each organization centers its activities on certain core processes that differenti-ate it in terms of their customer service, sales and marketing, product development, or other critical activity. The very importance of these processes to the organization suggests that they may be areas of focus for encapsulation within *process-focused components*.

It is unlikely that each process thread in the BPM will be supported by a dif-ferent component; some may be manual. Instead, a range of processes will have some of their most complex activities supported by a component. The process hierarchy can help with the identification of suitable groups of threads. For example, a bank will have many processes focused on supporting the adminis-tration of accounts for customers; these processes are central to the bank in terms of encouraging customer loyalty and helping the bank to attract new cus-tomers. The importance of these processes implies that they are likely to appear as a process group in the hierarchy. A 'customer account services' component may be an appropriate element of the architecture with responsibility for con-trolling the complex parts of these processes.

Responsibilities

Responsibilities are implied by the interactions described in the use cases. For example, the use case describing system response 'system displays a list of book-ings for the customer' clearly implies a responsibility to 'retrieve a list of bookings held by a specified customer'. Responsibilities are identified by looking for *verb clauses* in the descriptions of the use cases. Business processes can also provide useful input, but take care to ensure that the responsibilities are in the scope of the project; they might relate to purely manual activities.

Simply identifying the responsibilities is not enough to help with the creation of the business architecture. Can the responsibilities be grouped according to some set of appropriate criteria? The responsibility 'compute new balance' can probably be assigned to a group of responsibilities associated with the concept of sales. In contrast, which group would contain 'retrieve a list of bookings held by a specified customer'? The decision might be sales, or customer.

Information

Just as certain core processes are key to the continued success of the organization, certain key items of *information* are central to the execution of those processes. If the information is central to the execution of the process, it will be mentioned in the BPM and the use cases that support the processes. Using the above example, it is clear that information about sales and customer is certainly central to the solution being designed. Less significant items of data, e.g. customer name, also give clues about the core concepts to which they relate.

Key information items are identified by considering the information consumed and produced by the processes modeled in the BPM. Additional items of information can be identified by looking for *nouns* in the descriptions of the business processes,[7] use cases and other statements of requirements.

Once the core information has been identified, it can be used to form an *information model* for the solutions; Figure 5.8 shows an example. Each major concept can be represented as a class, and each less significant item of data can be an attribute of a class (or a relationship between classes). Showing the relationships between the classes refines the information model. Descriptions of the classes and attributes help to form a glossary of the information to be manipulated by the solutions.

Bringing it all together

The process, responsibility, and information views carry subtly different emphases, resulting in different groupings being derived. Consider the *coherence* of each of the groups: a highly coherent group of responsibilities may use less coherent groups of information. In this case, should the emphasis be on the large responsibility grouping, the smaller information grouping, or somewhere between the two? These differences must be reconciled in order to arrive at a coherent and consistent set of candidate components.

Also consider the *coupling*[8] between the groups. Loosely coupled groups of information may turn out to be tightly coupled in terms of responsibility. This

---

7. When using business processes, ensure that the noun is within the scope of the project and is not the subject of purely manual activity or incidental to the system.
8. Coupling defines the degree of linkage between elements.

Figure 5.8
Example of an information model

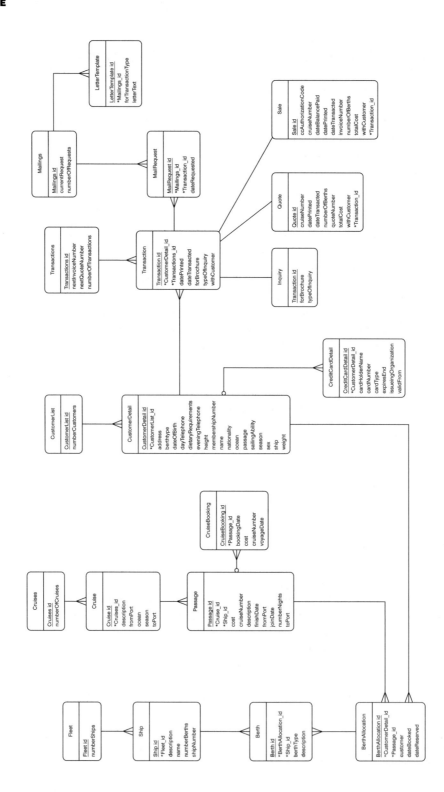

conflict can be resolved by merging the groups, or by introducing an element of process control between the two components. Perhaps a 'natural' process control has already been identified from the consideration of the business processes, for example the sales component.

Once a consistent set of the candidate components has been identified, these can be added to the information model as packages. Classes identified as being managed by each component can be shown inside the relevant package and scoped to it. The responsibilities identified for each component can be documented. Each package can be given a stereotype reflecting its origin as a process controller or information manager. However, many components will have a hybrid nature, in which case their main origin should be indicated by the chosen stereotype.

Whatever the complexities of deriving a consistent set of candidate components, do not spend too long on this activity. Remember, these are candidate components – their definitions will be refined as the design is elaborated, and there will inevitably be a degree of change in the business architecture.

First-time acquisition

Now that a set of candidate components has been identified, an opportunity exists to start using or reusing existing components or services, i.e. consuming them from the component repository. The component repository can be searched for existing components that manage processes, responsibilities, or information identified during the analysis. If suitable components are identified, their specifications can be reused from the component repository.

As web services may be used for both technical and business services, consideration of a dynamic 'plug and play' version for a solution can be made. This involves an initial decision as to whether to build a component or service, procure a component, procure a service, or reuse an existing internal component or service. If web services are to be used, then a service-level agreement that meets the required level of quality must be agreed with each service provider.

The boundaries of the reused components will probably differ, at least in detail, from those of the identified candidate components. This difference leads to a refactoring of the candidate component boundaries and a redefinition of the information and responsibilities they manage. It is even possible that these changes will reveal additional opportunities for reuse from the component repository. An important impact of acquiring components so early in the development process is that the business architecture used by the solutions is more closely aligned to other solutions already in use in the organization.

Components introduced by this approach will not usually include an information view, as they are specified as black boxes. Instead, the components' interfaces are available showing the services offered by the component. Those components that have not been used successfully have one or more service interfaces added to them to act as placeholders for services identified in the next stage. The number of interfaces chosen depends on how many groups of responsibilities have been assigned to the candidate component.

The result of the these activities is a set of *candidate business components*, which form the business architecture model.

Specify business component

To complete the external specification of the component, the candidate component's services must be identified and documented. To specify the services, the interactions between the user interface and the business components and between the business components themselves are considered. These interactions are described in the use cases, which form the hub of the requirements model and, to a lesser extent, in the more complex business rules.

Identifying services

For each use case, a UML sequence diagram is drawn; Figure 5.9 shows an example. Text on the left of the sequence diagram provides clear link to the use case – the structure follows that of the use case: wherever possible wording is reused too. Interactions modeled on the right show the invocation of services on the components defined in the business architecture. If components have been reused from the component repository, many services will be predefined; including these services in an interaction is early evidence of a correct reuse decision. Other services will be newly defined, representing services to be added to existing or new components.

Initially, the sequence diagram is kept simple by modeling only the basic course; subsequent elaboration adds extra interactions and services required to support the alternative courses. At all times, it is important to maintain a balance between the textual and interaction parts of the diagram. As services are created, the documentation for each new service is minimal – typically little more than the name of the service and a brief description of its objectives.

The result of this activity is both service descriptions of all the candidate business components and a verification of the steps in the use cases.

Workflow control

Process control is facilitated by specialized business components whose responsibilities include managing significant stages of important business processes. Complex use cases may also warrant the introduction of another type of control: the flow through the use case. One such example is FindCustomerDetailController in Figure 5.9.

Workflow controllers arbitrate between the interactions of the user and the service requests on specific business components and help to marshal the sets of data between the services. In analysis terms, they help to identify the units of interaction between the user and the system. In architectural terms, they simplify communication across the logical user and business tiers. Note that the analysis value of these controllers is sufficient justification for introducing them; they may have no physical equivalent in the implementation of the solution. Workflow controllers should be introduced only where the complexity of the use case interaction justifies their inclusion.

Figure 5.9
Example of a component service sequence diagram

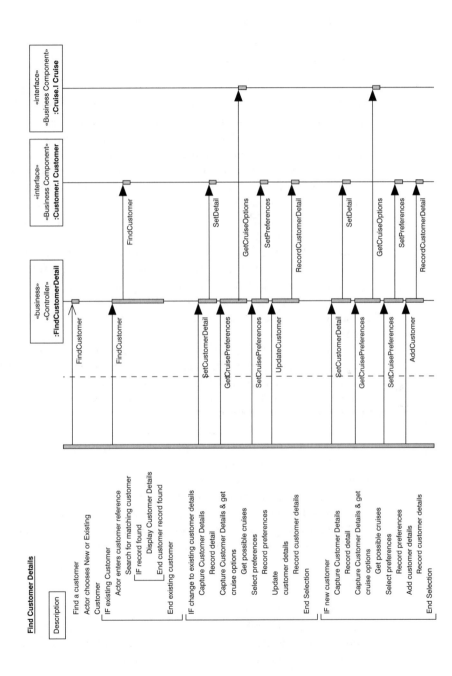

Business service specification

Service specification needs to consider:

- *business rules*: cross-referencing rules to services that need to evaluate them;
- *service granularity*: cohesion of individual services and coupling between services;
- *service protocols*: patterns of services that need to be invoked;
- *information requirements*: sets of data passed and returned by the service;
- *technical architecture*: ensuring standard parameters are included in the signature.

When the services have been identified, review them for their suitability in terms of coupling and cohesion. Are all the services cohesive?[9] If not, consider breaking a service up into smaller, more cohesive services. Refactoring of services in this way may lead to reuse; one of the new services forms a part of several original services. Are services tightly coupled (invocation of one service is consistently followed by invocation of another service)? If so, consider joining the services together into a single, larger service that reduces the number offered by a component.

Ultimately, refactoring services in this way may significantly change the component architecture. Components may be decomposed into smaller units to take account of enlarged, more specialized interfaces or aggregated into larger units to support larger-scale services. Reflect these changes in the information model and alter the scope of items in the information model to take account of the refactoring.

Protocols surrounding the use of services are specified by the *preconditions and post-conditions* associated with each service. Preconditions dictate what must be true about the application *before* the service can be invoked; they are similar to assumptions made by the service. Post-conditions state what will be different about the application *after* the service has completed its execution. Services may offer more than one set of post-conditions.

Complex services, those that help to drive significant business processes, may themselves have multiple courses of execution. The courses will depend on the results of intermediate services, their success or failure. Placing these interactions into a sequence diagram owned by the complex service can improve the structure of the model and simplify other sequence diagrams.

Once the component's services have been fully specified, it is now possible to detail the signatures: the input and output parameters.

Service signatures

Business services manage and transform business data owned by the components. They receive information entered by users or returned by other business services, and this information is processed according to the specified behavior of the service and other information is ultimately returned. This information

---

9. Their objective easily described in a single sentence, avoiding conjunction.

will subsequently be used by the user interface and by other services to continue the process. Documenting the information to be passed and returned by business services is a core specification activity.

Business services are at such a level that the volume of information received or returned may be significant. If every piece of information is passed as a separate parameter, the number of parameters will quickly become unmanageable. Structures offer a solution to this problem. Structures are groupings of related information that can be used to reduce the numbers of parameters on a service signature. Many structures will be shared between various services, even if the service does not use all the information in the structure. The use of structures is a modeling abstraction. Their implementation will depend on choices made within the technical architecture. A structure may be physically implemented in the code (e.g. as a 'typedef' or class), or it may be implemented using some other concept, such as an eXtensible Markup Language (XML) document and schema.

Technical architecture pervades all solutions when they are implemented. This architecture provides the environment within which the solution executes and facilitates communication between different elements of the solution. As a consequence, architecture needs to be 'designed in' to the business solution. Even very minimal technical architectures impose some requirements on the information passed when invoking a service. Typically, this information will include user and session identification, slots for passing error information, and so on. To specify this part of the service correctly, the designer must have a good understanding of the appropriate areas of the technical architecture and have access to the common structures, base classes and other deliverables provided by it. The technical architecture must have been designed, modeled, published and communicated.

Service tests

As services are specified, their *test cases* can be defined. Each test case describes the facet of the service being tested and specifies a set of data values to be passed as inputs and the data values expected to be received as results.

Service test cases can be associated with the test cases for a use case. Testing a specific scenario supported by a use case will imply the invocation of a pattern of services. Each service in the pattern will require a specific set of input data entered by the user or returned by previously invoked services, and produce a specific set of outputs to be consumed by services invoked later. If the scenario calls for a business error to be reported, the service that reports the fault must receive appropriate data during the test. Patterns of data used in service testing are not specified in isolation, as a chain of services can use the same pattern of data, thereby supporting the testing of use case scenarios.

Test specifications for web services will incorporate black-box tests only. Thought must be given to how external services may be tested or proved before implementation. This can involve building a stub for the web service that a test harness can use for initial system testing. But also consider the value of testing any procured services. Since the test itself may cost money, this is part of the value judgment when procuring the service and assessing the risk of not performing a particular test. Even one test may involve dealing with multiple service providers in the case of shared/replicated services.

The result of this activity is a set of test cases that will be run against the evolving component.

Component acquisition

Having specified the interface to the component, another attempt can be made at reusing components from the component repository. This time the search can be based on a more complete set of criteria, including the details of the services identified. If suitable components and services are found, they are consumed from the component repository into the model of the solution, replacing (or supplementing) the definitions of components already there. This activity leads to a restructuring of the component architecture and will probably require some of the interaction diagrams to be redrawn to take account of the new components.

If no suitable component can be found to meet the needs specified by the solution, or if components and services need enhancement, then the unmatched components need to be supplied in some way. Supply may be through buying components from a marketplace, contracting the development to a third party, wrapping existing heritage functionality, building a new component, or some combination of these activities. The choice of supply mechanism is usually at the discretion of the component management function or the supply-side teams. This supply process involves a negotiation between the suppliers and consumers of the newly specified component to finalize the services it will offer. The negotiation will also involve the prioritization and scheduling of the delivery of the requested services.

Summary

The business architecture defines the components and services that provide the business functions within the system. These components and their relationships are shown in the business architecture model and a supporting component information model. The services for each component are also defined. Even at this stage, the test cases for the component or service are specified. The main deliverables from this workflow are:

- business architecture model
- business component information model
- business component or service test specification.

Technical architecture

Technical architecture is a key requirement for the successful delivery of component-based solutions. Components must guarantee that they can 'inter-operate': coexisting and cooperating within a common technical environment. *Technical architecture* (Figure 5.10) is the workflow that ensures that a common technical environment is defined, communicated, reused, enhanced, and maintained across multiple projects.

Delivery of the technical architecture is achieved in two stages. In the first stage, the initial technical architecture is assembled and delivered. This is just like the execution of a normal CBD project, except that a *technical solution* is delivered rather than a business solution. This is known as the *technical architecture delivery*. However, this stage can be omitted if a technical architecture already exists and is suitable for the project.

In the second stage, the technical architecture is applied to multiple development projects; this is called *technical architecture integration*. As each project is executed, the technical architecture is assessed in terms of its fitness for purpose, gaps that must be filled, and additional technical issues introduced by the project. Over time, the technical architecture is extended and refined to meet the changing technical challenges presented by the development teams.

Technical architecture delivery

The technical architecture delivery is an application of the Select Perspective approach with the objective of implementing a *reusable technical architecture*. Technical architecture is expressed in the same terms as the design of a business solution, using UML diagrams and component models. As the name implies, technical architecture delivery involves the delivery of technical components and frameworks that support the use and maintenance of information (e.g. security and access control information) within the technical environment.

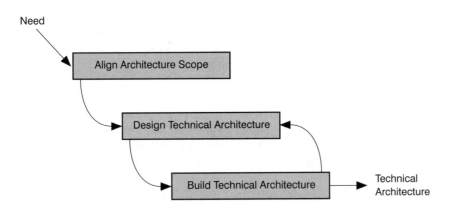

Figure 5.10
Technical architecture delivery workflow

The range of products delivered to support the technical architecture is wider than that delivered by a business solution project. In addition to operational solutions and their associated designs, technical architecture includes the concepts of *base classes*, *facility classes*, and *patterns* in its definitions. Solutions delivered by the technical architecture will include technical components that need to exist to support the business solutions; these may include security and access control, and error reporting. Each solution consists of the components that provide the technical services and the user interface functionality required to maintain the supporting information, such as an individual user's access rights.

Other deliverables do not take the form of fully operational software:

- *Facility classes*[10] are implemented to provide small-scale but frequently needed functionality. In contrast to a base class or pattern, the behavior required from facility classes can be completely specified so that the facility class can be fully implemented. It may be helpful to view a facility class as a small-scale, frequently reused component.

- *Base classes* are incomplete classes from which other classes will be derived. The base classes implemented by the technical architecture often reflect the architecturally derived stereotypes (business, user, controller, data) that will be used in the design of business solutions. A base class is usually partially implemented; basic behavior is provided for the stereotype modified or extended by specific classes used to implement a solution or component.

- *Patterns* are less concrete still. A pattern is a generic description of *how* a problem can be solved. The designer takes the pattern and applies it to the context in which they are working. The context may serve to alter the structure or content of the pattern to some extent. Patterns can be viewed as learning aids, as they document the typical way that a given problem is solved within the organization. Designers can use the pattern as a basis for solving their problem but adjust it as appropriate to fit the specifics of the situation.

Technical architecture requirements

The technical architecture is designed to support the technical needs of the business solutions that are being delivered and will be delivered in the future. Any requirements are therefore derived from the requirements of the business solutions. More specifically, the technical architecture requirements are based on the non-functional needs of the business solutions.

If the planned business solutions must be available 24/7, then data mirroring, automatic fail-over, and redundancy must be included in the capabilities of the technical architecture. If web solutions are to be supported, then web technology must be included in the technical architecture. If information state must be managed by the business components, then our delivery vehicle must support state-full components, or the technical architecture must define mechanisms by

---

10. Refer to www.selectbs.com for more details on facility classes in technical architecture.

which state-full behavior can be emulated. Many of these non-functional requirements will be readily identifiable during the *business alignment* workflow of a business project, where business process modeling can be a valuable source of non-functional requirements.

If a web services-based application is being considered, then build/rent/ reuse/buy decisions should be made for all aspects of the technical architecture.

The requirements for the technical architecture are expressed as *use cases*. However, these use cases are specialized from the normal usage and are referred to as *technical use cases*. Technical use cases may cover such interactions as 'start using a solution', 'user identification and access control', and so on. System interactions such as 'make component information persistent' and 'handle an error' will also be included.

Technical architecture design

From the technical use cases, interaction diagrams can be drawn (see Chapter 9). These are expressed in terms of the stereotypical elements of a business solution rather than in terms of specific classes. Thus an interaction diagram may include classes representing generic UI forms or controls, a generic business component interface, and so on. Many of these generic elements will be used to define the base classes.

Some elements modeled in the interaction will be specific. These are the elements that will eventually form an implemented part of the technical architecture, defined as service interfaces to the technical components and the facility classes.

To form the technical architecture patterns, the current model is effectively 'inverted'. Interaction diagrams as they are currently drawn show all the elements necessary to achieve one form of interaction such as error handling. An 'inverse' interaction diagram documents a technical pattern showing how one element (or small combination of elements) will be used in *all* interactions. These patterns aid the solution and component developers by giving them a ready source of material where they can find all the detail related to a single element of the technical architecture. Patterns typically form the basis of the published documentation for the technical architecture.

Testing the technical architecture

Having put so much effort into the design and construction of a technical architecture, it must be tested to ensure that it can deliver on its underlying requirement. However, initial tests cannot be executed through a business solution, since no business solutions will be available. It is therefore common practice to create a *test harness* to exercise the technical architecture. Sometimes the test harness will be based on some of the functional requirements of a specific business solution.

Training

Delivering the technical architecture is only half the battle. As with all other forms of reusable asset, the key to success is a high level of reuse. Solution and component teams must be educated in the content, application, and use of the technical architecture and its services. These teams must have sufficient knowledge to understand the technical resources available to them, both to prevent them from reinventing the wheel, and to apply each of the technical resources in an effective and appropriate manner.

Technical architecture delivery provides the common framework and components for the planned environments.

Technical architecture integration

We cannot totally predict the needs of future business solutions, so our technical architecture must continue to evolve alongside the business and technology choices. The *technical architecture integration* process focuses on taking the existing technical architecture, refining and improving it so that it provides better support for the business solutions currently in development.

Refinements include adding new features to the technical architecture up to and including the addition of whole new technologies: for example, the addition of web capabilities to support the first web-enabled solution in an organization. Changes of this scale are likely to be planned as incremental technical architecture deliveries (as described above).

The typical situation involves smaller-scale change to the technical architecture. For example, customer relationship management (CRM) solutions may require better response times than have previously been supported for other types of solution. The impact of this need on the technical architecture must be assessed in terms of both its requirements and the scale of the change. This change ranges from simplistic solutions such as buying bigger and better hardware through to more complex solutions, perhaps involving a transition from stateless to state-full components, with new patterns and other products being developed and tested.

Filling the gaps

Again, the requirements for the technical architecture come from the requirements of the business solutions that it must support. These requirements are evaluated in terms of the known capabilities of the existing technical architecture to identify the gaps that must be filled. Given the current model of the technical architecture, the impact of these gaps can be assessed in terms of the technical architecture patterns and proposed changes.

These changes are then prioritized and delivered on an incremental basis to match the delivery priorities of the business solution project. Testing the new capabilities will often be performed on early increments of the business solution itself, helping to confirm the accuracy of the gap analysis and the quality of the choices made.

Summary

Supplying a technical architecture is key to the successful delivery of component- or service-based solutions. Delivery of the technical architecture is achieved in two stages. In the first stage, the initial technical architecture is assembled and delivered; this is known as the *technical architecture delivery*. In the second stage, the technical architecture is applied to the project. The architectural framework is assessed, any gaps are filled, and new technical issues are resolved. This is called *technical architecture integration*.

The main deliverables from this workflow are:

- technical architecture specification
- technical architecture patterns
- technical component or service
- technical component or service usage guidelines
- base and facility classes.

Solution delivery

The business and technical architecture stages now move to *solution delivery*. Without the delivery of a solution, the stages that have gone before deliver little or no practical value. Delivery in this context means delivery into and through acceptance testing, with the final rollout of the solution into the operational environment being treated as a discrete workflow. Solution delivery focuses on the creation of the business solution in increments, with each increment realizing a prioritized value-adding group of use cases.

Figure 5.11 shows the major activities of the solution delivery workflow and how a *solution architecture* is central to all the activities. The solution architecture provides a comprehensive overview of the structure of the proposed solution. It is an analysis model that may be seen as the blueprint for the solution. Following completion of the solution architecture, the solution itself can then be implemented as a series of incremental deliveries of the solution, each of which will have its own *solution model*. As such, the solution architecture model covers the breadth of requirements – functional and non-functional – collated for the solution.

During design of the solution, relevant parts of the technical architecture are consumed into the model; examples include base classes for elements of the user interface and to provide control within the user interface. Technical components can also be consumed, especially those associated with security and error management. The solution architecture is refined during each increment, should each new use case introduce significant additional technical needs.

Figure 5.11
Solution delivery
workflow

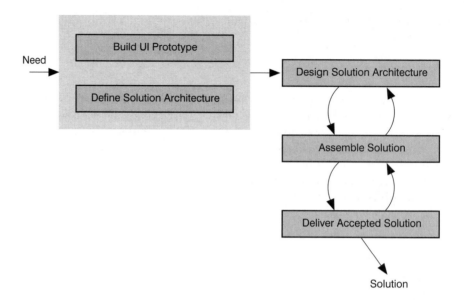

Build user interface prototype

Constructing a *user interface prototype* early in the project can help to identify the needs of the solution architecture. A clear understanding of the complexity of the user interaction will confirm the need for user interface control classes, e.g. interface controllers. Working iteratively between the use cases and the user interface prototype helps to ensure the completeness and consistency of both views.

Each use case[11] already has an associated interaction diagram[12] that shows the business services required from the components. During solution design, these interaction diagrams are refined to include components or services from the technical architecture and key elements of the user interface that the use case requires, e.g. screen forms. Refinements introduced at this stage may affect the flow of the user interaction, necessitating changes to the documentation of the courses in the use case. Ultimately, the structure of the use case model itself may be altered to show any extraction of suitable «include» or «extend» use cases. Changes are rarely needed to the business process model.

Code is constructed on a per use case basis. User interface, control, and other deliverables involved in the interaction are realized in code and unit tested by the developer. Delivered code is linked to the business services, which may be 'stubbed'[13] at this point. Each developer takes responsibility only for the functionality required by the use case they are working on. If a coder creates a component but only needs some of its capabilities, the remainder will be

---

11. Delivered through the business alignment workflow.
12. Delivered through the business architecture workflow.
13. Stubbing is when a component or class interface is provided with simple code that performs no logic other than accepting the request and, if required, returning known data.

defined as 'stubs' to be completed later, perhaps by other coders. Available services can be tested through the user interface for the first time.

When all the use cases in the increment have been constructed and unit tested, they can be integrated into a deliverable unit. After integration testing, the packaged increment can be delivered into the acceptance test environment for testing by the user community or their representatives. Faults will always be uncovered during acceptance testing. Each fault will be the target of rework as necessary; significant faults may require more extensive corrective work to be scheduled, causing an impact on the scope and planning for the next increment.

At the end of each increment, priorities are reviewed and adjusted to maintain alignment between priorities and the business solution. Increments continue to be delivered until all the requirements have been implemented, or the project exhausts it timescales or budget.

Define solution architecture

User interface technology must be capable of supporting the user requirement. One option is to select from technology already used in the organization. However, balance needs to be achieved between supporting the requirement and imposing too great a level of complexity on the user community. Any architectural choices must be agreed with the user community. For example, are they happy with a web-based interface rather than a traditional client–server interface?

Gap analysis is undertaken to determine shortfalls between the organization's technologies and the presentation needs dictated by the proposed solution. Significant shortfalls may impose additional requirements and constraints on the technical architecture, resulting in the addition of new capabilities to the technical architecture. In more extreme cases, new or updated technologies will be adopted. If sufficient new technology is being adopted, it is appropriate to produce a *thin-slice prototype* from selected use cases in the solution to prove both the technology and the delivery capability of the project team. As with technical architecture, web services may also have an impact on the solution architecture.

Many solutions need to interface with other systems, perhaps legacy systems that must continue in operation and are not suited to componentization or systems offered by third parties. The detailed interaction with these external entities requires design in order to complete the solution architecture. On the solution side, each of the external entities will be implemented as a *wrapper* that provides the functionality through a service-based interface so that these entities appear to be a component. Services required through the wrapper have already been identified as part of the business architecture; however, the detailed implementation of the wrapper must be designed to confirm that the requirements can be met.

Design solution architecture

Earlier stages of the *consume* process have laid down the business architecture, and solution design makes this initial architectural view more detailed and concrete so that it can be implemented as executable code. Design starts with documenting the requirements with use cases and interaction diagrams, then specifying the tests.

Design of the solution proceeds on a per use case basis. In each increment, a group of use cases is selected for delivery. These use cases, or parts of use cases such as the basic or key alternative courses, are designed, constructed, integrated, and subsequently tested.

Design of a use case has already started. An interaction diagram showing the pattern of invocation of services has been constructed as part of the business architecture. This high-level design is made more concrete so that code can be constructed from it. From the parts of the user interface prototype relevant to the use case, key elements such as forms, server pages, or control classes are selected. These elements are represented as appropriately stereotyped classes in the solution model and are presented on a class diagram; Figure 5.12 shows an example.

Consuming software assets is not restricted to business components. Elements of the user interface can be published as components for future reuse within the supply–manage–consume environment. UI elements will range in scale from widgets to complex sub-windows capable of presenting important recurring information. Many of the smaller, simpler elements will be bought from third-party suppliers, perhaps via the component marketplace.

Each of these different elements is added to the original interaction diagram to show the interactions between all elements; Figure 5.13 shows such an example. Patterns of behavior in the user interface will be identified, including the flow of form or page presentation, and the change of state of individual controls

Figure 5.12
Example of a user interface class diagram

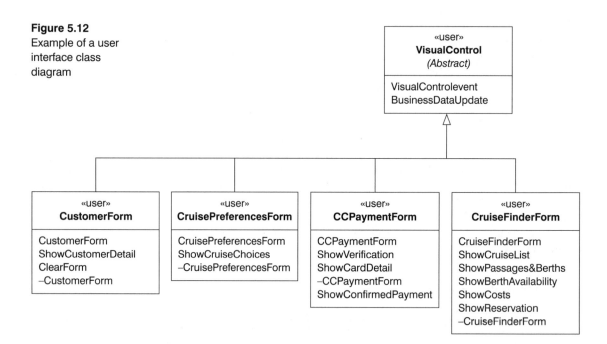

Figure 5.13
Example of a solution design object sequence diagram

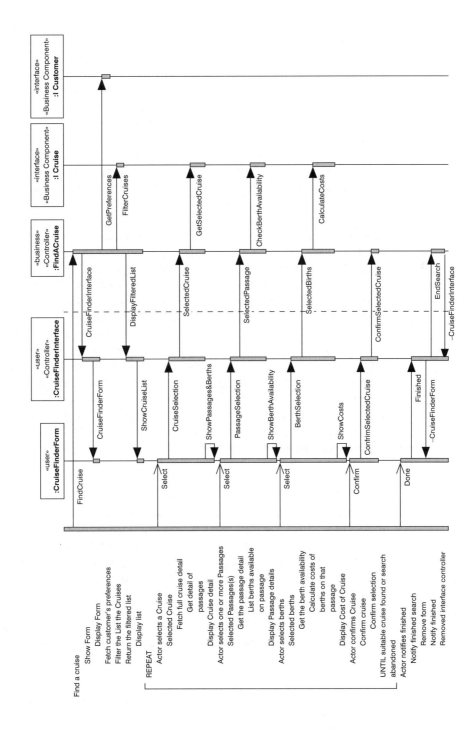

or areas of the interface. Units of interaction, identified during the initial modeling of the use case, will be refined. These typically become smaller as the design of the user interface reveals opportunities for decomposition. For example, the retrieval of the details of a customer, their account, orders and so on may initially be modeled as a single user interaction. The user interface may indicate the use of a tabbed control, allowing different facets of customer information to be retrieved as the different tabs are selected.

Items from the technical architecture model are also added to the class and interaction diagrams. These include base and facility classes, from which UI elements are derived (see Figure 5.12) and services to be invoked by the user interface, for example to manage security, authorization, and error reporting. Technical architecture patterns are also used to form the solution model, which can lead to re-factoring of the interaction to make use of relevant patterns.

State change diagrams can also be used to indicate how elements of the solution architecture change their behavior in response to changes in internal state or the passage of time. For example, areas of a UI will be enabled or disabled depending on the results of user activity such as searching for information; a successful search for customers results in the customer list area of a panel being enabled. Control objects may also be state-sensitive, the flow of UI activity depending on the results of each action as it is executed.

The solution design must take the state model and decide how the elements expressed in the model will be implemented. Facilities provided by the technical architecture have a strong influence on these decisions. Choices such as how events are handled are guided by the technical architecture model, which shows the facilities inherent in the implementation environment, or built into a UI base class, or by specific private operations added to the UI class itself. Use of state variables or specific methods to evaluate state will also be guided by the technical architecture.

Design test cases

All designers are responsible for creating test cases that will exercise specific paths through the use case (see Chapter 9). These white-box[14] test cases prove that the code itself operates in accordance with the detailed design. All test cases are based on existing cases created and documented for each use case, but with more detail added showing how the data are transformed by specific sections of the code.

At the end of these activities, the business components have been combined with the user interface elements and the technical architecture components and services. Test cases have been designed for all the components and services.

---

14. White-box testing is testing that exercises the code on a line-by-line basis; in contrast, black-box testing exercises the unit only in terms of its inputs and outputs and does not examine the detailed implementation.

Assemble solution

Construction and integration of the solution once again proceeds on a per use case basis, with each use case representing a potentially usable segment of the functionality of the system. Each developer/developer team takes responsibility for delivering a planned set of the use cases. Design and construction of use cases can often be managed very effectively using principles such as the use of 'buddy teams',[15] espoused by the agile process community [Beck].

Construction of the components required by the use case is driven from the interaction model created during design. Components used in the interaction are generated from the model if they are not already present in the source code configuration. This generation process creates skeletal versions of all of the public operations to be offered by each class; some code may need to be added to the implementation of each operation or method in order to provide effective code stubs. Once the code has been generated, the developer concentrates only on elaborating the methods actually required by the design of the interaction (the other methods will be elaborated as other use cases are constructed). The structure of each method is explicit in the interaction diagram. Some complex or frequently reused methods may even have their own interaction diagrams detailing method-specific behavior.

The developer must also take account of state-based behavior. The state change diagrams show how the elements of the solution architecture change their behavior in response to changes in state or the passage of time. Event handlers must be constructed in accordance with the business level design and the mechanisms prescribed by the technical architecture. Construction covers all of the deliverables described in the use case interaction that need to be created or extended. Deliverables include elements of the user interface, control elements and those derived from the technical architecture (base and facility classes, and interfaces to technical components), and the interfaces to the business components are integrated during construction.

It is common for such construction to take place in *sandboxes*. Sandboxes are development and testing areas allocated to an individual developer, or a small group of developers. These sandboxes allow programming, compilation, linking, testing, etc. to be undertaken without impacting other developers. When the construction work is completed and tested to the developer's satisfaction, then the deliverables are submitted for unit testing.

Unit test

Following the principles of high quality and empowerment espoused by the agile methods community, the developer's responsibility does not end with the delivery of code that simply compiles. Each developer is responsible for

---

15. One buddy taking responsibility for design and the other being responsible for construction proves particularly productive.

delivering code that operates in accordance with the specification and design. If that code has been developed (and tested) in a sandbox, then the code will be integrated with other parts of the solution before the test cases are executed. To execute the tests, the developers need to access data, which may be achieved through the creation or extraction of specific test data or through the provision of proxy data objects.[16] If web services are being used, then either 'live' services will need to be used to support the testing, or some kind of dummy service may need to be implemented.

Working as a team, designers and developers use the test results to correct any design issues that become apparent as the code is constructed and tested. Construction of the use case is considered to be complete when all the code to support the use case has been created and tested by the team.

Deliver accepted solution

Before a solution delivery can be made to, or accepted by, its recipient, it is necessary that the tests defined for it are executed in accordance with the *test plan* for the delivery. If these tests are acceptable, then the tested solution is assembled into a deployable solution package for delivery into the *solution roll-out process*.

Part of the test plan is the *user acceptance test specification*, which describes the complete set of test cases for the delivered system. These can be of the following forms:

● *Functional tests*, based on proving the successful completion of specific use cases. These ensure that the system provides the required functionality and operates as expected.

● *Usability and ergonomic tests* explore the person/machine interface to ensure that it is comprehensive, consistent, and understandable. Clarity is needed for both the operations and the error reports and messages from the system.

● *User documentation tests* are similar to the ergonomic tests, except that they are focused on matching the system behavior to the user documents.

The user acceptance tests should map directly from the functional requirements of the system (expressed as use cases). Their purpose is to ensure that the services to be provided by the system work as expected, and according to non-functional requirements such as usability and performance. Usability testing is one of the most important elements of user acceptance testing.

Once the test environment has been installed or initialized, then a series of test cases are executed. These tests determine whether the deliverable elements of a given solution delivery satisfy the functional, non-functional and other requirements defined for them.

---

16. An object that returns known, fixed data to the calling object instead of accessing database tables; a substitute data table.

Summary

Solution delivery is the creation and assembly, through acceptance testing, of the business solution in a series of increments. The main deliverables from this workflow are:

- user interface prototype
- solution architecture model
- solution model
- solution build
- solution release.

Solution rollout

During the solution delivery process, a number of releases are delivered at the end of most increments. But only a few of these releases will be rolled onto the operational platform for use by the business users. For example, the early increment releases may be proving the technical architecture solution, the user interface interaction, the database structures, a thin-slice prototype, and so on.

The rollout of the solution can vary significantly depending on the distribution and nature of the user base. In the unlikely event that it is a 'greenfield' implementation, rollout can occur with less user disruption but will still require deployment and user training activities. In the real world, there may also be legacy data and applications to be integrated or migrated.

Given the impact of any rollout of the solution, careful planning and specification are needed and should be started early in the project, i.e. in parallel with other workflows. One of the major decisions is on the *migration strategy*: big bang versus incremental migration. Big-bang migration is at least relatively easy to understand in terms of its outcome: it either succeeds, in which case the new solutions come into use, or it fails, when a fallback strategy is adopted. However, big-bang migration puts all the risk into one basket; apparent success may mask very real failures, which may become apparent only during continuing operation. Big-bang migration can also be extremely difficult to schedule, as the amount of time taken to migrate large volumes of data – during which operations must effectively cease – is a very real problem. Finding large enough gaps in operating schedules can lead to very hard deadlines for solution delivery: either rushing to completion if the deadline is tight or delaying business benefit if the deadline is distant.

Incremental migration provides the opportunity to manage risk effectively and allows more flexibility in the rollout of the new solution. However, incremental migration is much more difficult to plan. For example, how are the increments to be structured: vertical slices through the architecture or horizontal slices through the data, or some combination of the two? How will referential integrity within the partially migrated architecture be maintained? Issues such as these need to be addressed when planning incremental migration.

Once the operational procedures, migration strategy, and test plans are in place, solution releases can be rolled out onto delivery systems and the training of users can begin.

Figure 5.14 outlines the key steps, which are:

1 *Establish operational procedures*: develop the procedures to be executed during the rollout of the solution, including how the software is to be released and maintained.

2 *Define operational test plan*: define the operational tests to be executed against the solution rollout test environment before rollout can progress.

3 *Build solution release*: build and test the solution for rollout onto delivery systems.

4 *Deploy release*: take the completed release and deploy this to the client, application and database servers and mainframe machines.

5 *Rollout training*: implement user training for all users involved in the solution rollout.

Establish operational procedures

Operational procedures are complex and detailed as they include the release procedures, content, acceptance criteria, and error handling. If a smaller, simpler solution is being rolled out, then the amount of detail in each of the procedures is reduced. However, it is recommended that each of the procedures be considered carefully, even to noting 'no action', to be certain that the rollout is successful.

The *release procedures* define the required support for managing issues that arise during the release of the installation into the production environment. These ensure that disruption of the production environment is minimized and that the installation proceeds as smoothly as possible. *Service-level agreements* are established to ensure that the procedures can be executed in the timescales available. It is usually necessary to fully specify the content, software deliverables, and

Figure 5.14
Solution rollout
workflow

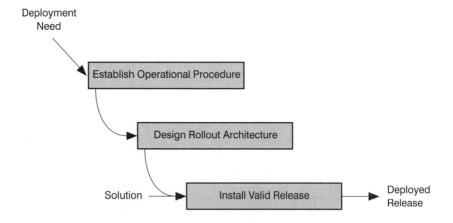

dependencies of the release as part of the *release content*, as well as the *acceptance criteria* for issuing the release in terms of documentation to be provided, solution and system testing success levels, and configuration management labeling.

One essential element often overlooked is the *error recording procedures*. These define the levels of help desk availability – for example, 7/5 coverage and answerphone coverage at other times – as well as identifying and documenting the error notification and resolution process for errors found in the live release. This may also involve service-level agreements for the resolution and/or escalation of errors.

Solution operations procedures include solution and component start-up and shut-down, with any batch or automated facilities provided by the solution described in terms of execution, control, and management procedures. If using web services, the operational procedures need to consider liaison with the many external service providers.

Consideration must be given to data back-up and restoration procedures if these differ from the standard procedures. Once again, service-level agreements for the resolution of operational problems will be defined. As part of the operations, *disaster recovery procedures* identify and document the procedures necessary to implement the solution package in the organization's disaster recovery architecture.

Identify training needs

The success of any new software solution is dependent upon its use by the user base. The easy and productive use of a solution is directly related to the capability of the users, who are reliant upon appropriate training and support. This activity identifies the required training for the successful rollout of the solution and delivers this to the training department/function that will execute the *training plan*.

To determine the user training needs, the planned solution is first reviewed against existing procedures and software systems to produce a *process change list*, which documents any changes to the manual operations. Then scenario workshops are conducted with business representatives to review all the use cases in the solution to determine the required training elements for these users to use the system successfully in a 'live' environment. Consideration is also given to the *media* for each training requirement, e.g. workshop, computer-based training, or user guide.

The results of these activities are consolidated *training requirements documents* and a *training plan* for delivery of the required training media for the training requirements.

Define test specification

This activity defines the internal and external *test cases* for a given aspect of the system. These test cases are used to determine whether a specific deliverable (e.g. component, increment, or solution) meets the requirements defined for it. Multiple test specifications are used as input to the *test plan* for a delivery.

The test specification is defined and developed in parallel with the aspect of the system it is designed to test. It should become comprehensive by the time the system element is complete. The steps involved are:

1 *Review test strategy* to ensure that the test strategy as currently defined meets the overall needs of the project.

2 *Refine test approach* to define or refine the approach to testing, given the priorities assigned to the services and the non-functional constraints being applied.

3 *Refine testing requirements* that document test setup procedures and locations of test data.

4 *Define test environment* suitable for testing the aspects of the system that are being specified. The test environment should be recoverable to its original state for accurate, repeatable testing. This also involves identifying testing tools and the means of testing (e.g. use of a test harness).

5 *Prepare test cases*, which evaluate the quality and suitability of the scope element being tested. Test cases contain activities to verify the particular element of the system to be tested. They can be combined into a *test suite*, which runs all tests of a specified type.

Prepare test cases

Definition of test cases is best done at the same time as the definition of requirements to be tested. This enables a much tighter definition of verifiable requirements, as each has to answer the question 'How can we prove or certify this?' The content of test cases can then be determined alongside the development of the functionality to be tested.

First, identify the major scenarios through which the scope element is to be tested; each course through the scope item will give rise to multiple test scenarios. Then specify how many tests should be executed for the course and the number of times the tests should be carried out. The quantification of the testing will depend on the priority assigned to the scope item and to the scenario tested. High-value, high-frequency items and scenarios should be tested more rigorously than low-value, low-frequency items.

Also incorporate tests for the non-functional requirements, as these apply to different scope items in the increment. These help to define additional tests, including security, load, speed, and reliability tests, that must be applied to specific scope elements.

One or more test cases are written to exercise the scenario. Each test case describes the steps that must be taken and information that must be provided as input and the expected results derived from the execution of a step. For use cases, the steps are derived from the interaction diagram, which details the interaction between the user and the system. For services offered by components, the service design interaction diagram can be used.

These activities result in a set of *operational documents* that cover the operation and testing of the rollout.

Define operational test plan

This defines the operational tests to be executed against the solution rollout test environment before rollout can progress. This also tests the error-recording process and the skills of the individuals allocated to the error-resolution process.

As the delivery can consist of multiple deliverables, the *test plan* will draw test cases from multiple test specifications. In the process of defining the tests new requirements can be uncovered. Different types of testing will be required at different points in the development cycle. The test plan draws on test cases defined for:

- *component testing*, to verify the quality of components;
- *solution testing*, to verify the quality of whole or part solution deliveries;
- *user acceptance testing*, to verify that the functional requirements have been met and that the system is usable;
- *operational testing*, to verify the non-functional and management requirements of the solution.

Depending on what is being tested, the test plan will incorporate the necessary test approach and test environment to enable the ensemble of test cases to be executed.

If you are using web services, then user acceptance testing should use the live environment. But there should be no need to consider the impact of using a web service on any other users of the service, e.g. other businesses. If the service provider has signed up to supporting 10,000 concurrent users, it should be of no consequence whether those users are real or simulated. If 10,000 simulated users cause denial of service for other users, then things will not get better when the application goes live.

Build release

This activity creates the release of all the required software and operating system elements plus the solution and installs and/or deploys this into the operational environment, e.g. client, server, and mainframe machines. As integration of web services require integration testing with *live* web services, the go-live date for the web services should predate the final go-live date for the application. This allows stress testing of each service before going live.

The first step is to identify all the software, solution, component, technical architecture, and operating system elements to be installed/deployed for the build and the nodes to which they must be deployed. This may mean building the database and any data importation/migration and the generation procedures to be included in this build. The *build scripts/deployment files*, which define the correct deployment locations, must also be created. These scripts/files are then executed to construct the deployable software elements and deployed onto the selected hardware nodes. Any issues with the build and deployment that arise are recorded, together with any corrections or workarounds.

Perform operational tests

The source and result data for the test are gathered then compared with the expected inputs and outputs documented in the test. All documented test actions are performed and results compared with the documented test results; any issues arising from the comparison are recorded. The outcome of the test is then decided and recorded based on the evaluation of the input and result data against acceptance criteria, with responsibility for the resolution assigned for any issues that must be resolved.

When this has been completed, a final assessment of the quality of the operational element is made and, depending on the impact of the operational element, a decision is made as to whether it can proceed to rollout or it should be removed from the rollout.

Deploy release

With all the pre-planning and testing complete, deployment is now a straightforward activity involving execution of the build scripts/deployment files to construct the deployable software elements and deployment onto the selected operational hardware nodes and migrating data from the agreed baseline database into the production environment. Any issues that arise with the build and deployment, including any corrections or workarounds, are recorded.

Rollout training

This activity implements training for all users involved in the solution rollout. This means identifying the groups of users, from target business users and system operators, to be trained through specific training media such as workshops, or computer-based training, and forming the schedule of training sessions.

To ensure that the training material is acceptable, conduct a dress rehearsal with selected business representatives, running through the training and gathering feedback on quality and effectiveness. Where negative feedback is received, prioritize the issues identified and refine the materials appropriately. Use the feedback received to validate the use and format of the feedback mechanisms.

Then execute the training to the business users following the agreed schedule. After each training event, examine the feedback received and, where necessary, conduct follow-up training or mentoring as appropriate. Update the training plan with progress and adjust the plans to take account of any additional training or retraining.

Summary

Only a few solution releases will be rolled onto the operational platform following the solution delivery process. However, the rollout must be planned early in the project, as the solution can vary significantly depending on the distribution and nature of the user base. For example, there may be legacy data and applications to be integrated or migrated. The main deliverables from this workflow are:

- operational documents
- operational test specification
- legacy migration plan
- solution release.

Maintain and support solution

This workflow, shown in Figure 5.15, provides resources that ensure the operational system continues to meet the needs of the business and its users by responding to requests for help, changes, and reports of failures. After evaluation, each selected request is allocated an owner and is added to the work schedule. System maintenance is as much a state of mind as a development phase. This is particularly true for incremental development, where an application is developed and delivered many times, and thus does not reach the maintenance state unless a specific decision is made. The solution will evolve continuously, meeting new business needs until a conscious choice is made to stabilize its functionality and place it 'into maintenance'.

Whether the application is 'in maintenance' or not, it still requires support. This can come in a number of forms:

- *user support*: helping users in their day-to-day use of the system;
- *issue management*: finding bugs and issues, and planning solutions and/or workarounds;
- *enhancement planning*: logging and prioritizing potential enhancements to the system.

When the application is still in development, enhancement planning is normally part of the project manager's remit in negotiation with the user community. Responsibility moves to the support manager when the solution is in maintenance. This change of responsibility recognizes that regular project

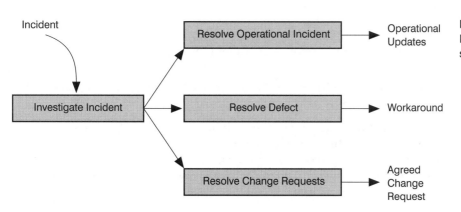

Figure 5.15
Maintain and support solution workflow

resources are no longer available to enhance the solution. Instead, resources must be allocated from the maintenance team, which is often much more limited in size and flexibility and where there is competition from other solutions already in maintenance. Major enhancements of the solution will normally be made the subject of a new project, for which a specific development team is assembled.

Solution support focuses on assisting the user community in their day-to-day use of the business solution once it is in operation. Central to the activity of the support area is capturing the details of *incidents* reported by users so that the performance of the solution can be improved and more closely aligned with the business needs. Not all incidents relate to the need to modify or correct the solution. Incidents arise simply because of lack of knowledge and expertise on the part of users. The provision of advice and guidance to the user will often resolve these issues, and if the lack of knowledge is more significant then new or additional training may be in order.

Other incidents may arise from known causes that are either already the target of corrective action or that have a documented *workaround* that permits users to continue their work. Keeping users informed about work schedules and the impact of known issues is important to maintaining confidence in the operation and use of the solution.

New issues

Some incidents will relate to issues that have not arisen before. These require investigation by the support team to determine the cause of the problem and to find a possible workaround. Results of the investigation are recorded so that information can be given to other users reporting the same issue. If the issue arises from a fault in the solution, or in the services supporting the solution, corrective action must be scheduled. When relying on web services, investigation may require support from one or more web service providers.

The mechanisms used to plan and execute the correction may differ depending on where the fault lies. Faults in the solution will be corrected by a solution maintenance team, which takes responsibility for the quality of service delivered by the operational solutions. The planning and scheduling of the corrective work will depend on:

- the severity and scope of the fault, e.g. does it always 'crash' the system;
- the impact of the fault on the organization, e.g. are the wrong prices being calculated.
- the current workloads within the maintenance teams, e.g. when can they get round to fixing this.

Faults originating from components and their services are often managed differently. The reuse of the services means that the impact of these faults is likely to be felt across more than one solution, so giving the fault a higher priority. Often the group responsible for the development of the components will retain responsibility for enhancement and maintenance of these assets. When using web services, as with any external provision of services, there is always the danger that the cause may not appear to lie with a given service provider or, in the worst case, that the service provider denies responsibility. To avoid this situation, ensure that comprehensive service-level agreements are in place.

The fault will be assigned to the component team; again the scheduling of the corrective action will depend on its severity, impact[17], and the current workload. A fault in a component service will have an impact on all the solutions that use it. Before any correction can be put into operation, all the affected solutions must be regression tested. Once the correction has been made operational, the benefit will be felt by all users of all of the affected solutions.

Enhancements

Issues will arise because the solution needs to evolve to retain its alignment to the ever-changing business processes it supports. The management of enhancement requests will depend on their scale and business impact. Minor enhancements may be treated in the same way as solution faults, although it will often be the case that work must be synchronized between the solution support and component teams.

More significant enhancements will be treated as additional projects, each project perhaps encompassing several enhancement issues. The development cycle effectively starts again, with a project team being formed and a full incremental and iterative project plan being executed.

Summary

Maintain and support provides resources that ensure the operational system continues to meet the needs of the business and its users by responding to requests for help, changes, and reports of failures. The main deliverables from this workflow are:

- incident log
- change request
- change schedule
- defect log
- risk register.

---

17. Design-time faults can be reduced through application of the *design-by-contract* technique (see Chapter 9).

Data architecture $\quad$ 6

The value of a system to an organization is realized by the data that is stored and the ways that the system is able to manipulate and present it as information. Processes add value by changing the state of information. It is clear that information is the lifeblood of the organization: information is power. Despite the fundamental importance of information, organizations deal with it in different ways and at different levels and scales of working: component, organization, and solution.

At the smallest scale, which is the *component scale*, information managed by a specific business component may be stored using a database that is equally specific. When working at this scale, the data should not be central to the core activities of the organization; the component may well focus on supporting the technical architecture, perhaps by providing error-handling services.

Very frequently, *solution-scale* data management is used. Most of the data are specific to a solution or small group of solutions, and can be managed effectively on this scale. Components underlying the solutions will share a common data architecture and have their data service requirements provided by one or more data components. Some data may be provided by other systems, probably by providing data services through the same data components.

If data central to the organization's operation is to be managed, it is likely that the solutions will have to share the data architecture with many other systems: *organizational scale*. The flexibility to create new structures or change existing structures within such architecture is clearly limited and will frequently act as a constraint on the new solutions. Data may be accessed by providing data services accessing the existing architecture or by wrapping functionality provided by the existing systems.

Data services are provided by data components, which act as a bridge between mainly business components and the database services (see definition of data component in Chapter 10). The major benefit of this separation of responsibilities is that changes in the business component structure or the database schema do not cause 'ripples' throughout the other structures,. Data components are delivered as part of the supply process, i.e. component delivery.

Whichever scale is appropriate, it is important to consider any existing data that may be involved. For example, a component may be being extended or updated, and the impact of the changes affect the existing data services or databases. The presence of existing data may constrain the planned updates to the component or solution.

The scale of the work involved in creating the data architecture will depend on the scale at which the solutions must integrate. Different scales can and will often be mixed within the same project. For example, to increase the flexibility of solutions to manipulate new data, a project may combine organizational-scale and solution-scale data architectures. The new elements of the data architecture will be designed and managed at solution scale. Unless the solution-scale elements conform to the existing architecture and adhere to organizational standards, further difficulties will arise when existing systems are extended to take account of the enhanced data architecture. Even though the new elements are being used only by the new solutions, they may have to be verified and agreed by the organizational DBA, data architect, and data authority (see Chapter 8).

To complicate matters further, the data architecture may have to span several potentially incompatible data environments. Solutions may be assembled from components that wrap legacy or COTS package functionality in combination with other more locally sourced data. From the components point of view, the data architecture is simple: all data access is mediated through data services. It is the data services that hide or encapsulate the complexity of multiply sourced data.

Data architecture delivery

Data architecture delivery takes the business architecture – a model expressed in logical terms – created by a project and ensures that this architecture conforms to the existing data architecture that the solutions must use. Gap analysis indicates shortcomings in the project's business architecture and where the existing data architecture may need to be extended to support the business requirement. Each item in the business architecture is assigned to one or more of the existing data environments, or is recognized as being something new that must be managed explicitly by the solution or used to extend an existing data environment.

The impact of changes from both functional and non-functional requirements must be assessed and proved by a cost–benefit analysis. If changes cannot be justified, the scope of the project will have to be adjusted, or a suitable mixed data architecture chosen for the project. In any case, the scheduling of changes to the data architecture (and the systems it supports) will have an impact on the planning of the development project.

The project business architecture is refined to resolve issues identified in the gap analysis. This will result in refactoring of component and service boundaries, requiring the solution team to adjust its designs accordingly. Component teams need to alter component designs to take into account the refactoring of the service interfaces. Design of data services[1] is based on the logical structures expressed in the refined business architecture.

Detailed design of the data architecture applies knowledge of each of the physical data environments, their capabilities and constraints, to create database structures that will meet the non-functional constraints imposed on the project. Except for agreed changes, the new designs must conform to the existing data implementation. If *data migration* is required, the design of the data environments must include the procedures, functions, and plans needed to execute the data migration. These procedures and functions must be tested to ensure a complete and correct migration of data. Regular transfer or synchronization of data between physical data environments may also be a requirement, which will impose additional constraints on the design of the data architecture.

Data architecture analysis

Data architecture analysis considers the structural needs of the solution and the contextual needs of existing architecture and systems in order to derive a strategy for a successful data implementation. Following this strategy, a logical view of the data architecture, expressed in terms and concepts familiar to the user community, is derived. The derivation of the logical view may be constrained by the chosen strategy, in particular by having to conform to existing, more global, data architectures.

Analyze information needs

The data authority works with the project team to gain a thorough understanding of the informational needs of the solutions. The derivation of these needs is based on the principles described in the business architecture section of the consume workflow. Using a combination of process, responsibility and information, an abstract view of the items of information needed by the solutions is formed. This view includes the attributes used to describe the items of information and the major relationships that exist between them. Considering the coupling and cohesion implied by the different starting points, the information items can be grouped into candidate components; see Figure 6.1.

The data architect's role in this activity is first to ensure that the work of the solution project conforms to any architectural standards already in place in the

---

1. Data services are considered to be a specialized form of component service, delivered by the use of specific processes and techniques within the component delivery workflow.

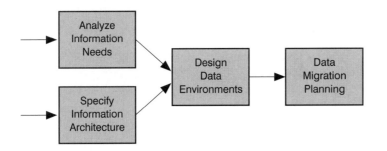

Figure 6.1
Data architecture
workflow

organization. However, it is very important to avoid constraining the analysis too much at this stage. Very often the data architect will assist by adding significant detail to the information model. This detail is based on their knowledge of the existing data architectures in the organization.

Throughout the analysis, the data architect will be able to provide information about the complexities and possible costs of the requirements being modeled. Complexity and cost are likely to increase significantly each time a new source of data is introduced into the project scope. The data architect will also be aware of other projects being executed concurrently, and be able to indicate where alignment with these projects could bring benefits and where conflicts need to be resolved. This may also apply to the services being developed in parallel, when it could be useful for the DBA to act as service librarian.

During information modeling, consideration is also given to the exchange of this information between the components themselves, in particular the information exchange across architectural or machine boundaries (see Figure 6.2). Contemporary systems exploit the XML standard for information exchange, in which data typing and schema organization are replaced by a structured character stream that is packed and unpacked by the data service components. This style of data formating allows flexibility and adaptability in information exchange.

Specify information architecture

Specification of the information architecture begins by analyzing the data requirements with respect to the importance of the solution to the organization, the scale (size and complexity) of the solution, and existing data architectures. Timescales, financial constraints, and the non-functional requirements of the project must also be taken into account.

The total strategy will be more complex than a simple statement of conformity. Gap analysis will reveal shortcomings in the business architecture of the solution project – elements of information that must be managed in order to maintain the integrity of the organization's data. The analysis will also indicate where new items of information are being called for. Each of the information elements must be assigned a location in one or more of the physical data environments within the information architecture.

Figure 6.2
Example of an information model

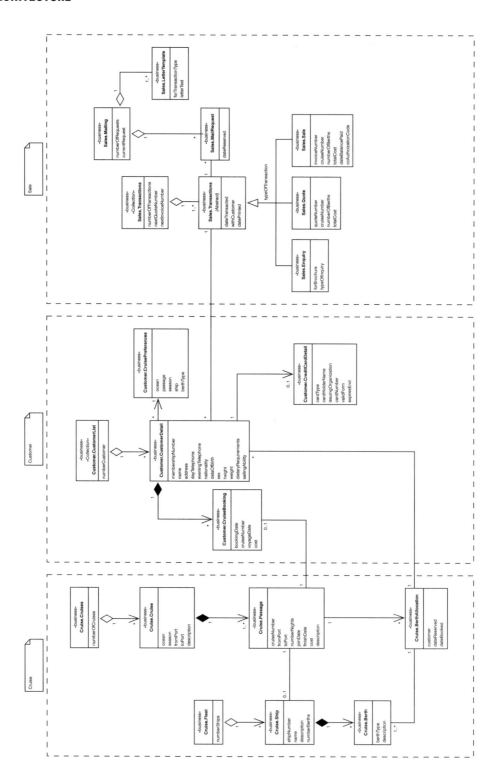

If there are extensions to the existing data architecture, then the strategy for managing these must be defined. If extensions are permitted, how will the impact on existing systems be managed? Will changes to systems be scheduled? If so, what will be the impact on the solution project's timescales? If not, then how will the mismatch in data architectures be handled? If extensions are ruled out, then significant functionality may have to be removed from the scope of the project, with consequent loss of functionality in the delivered solution.

The strategy must provide answers to these key questions, so that the agreed business architecture can be supported effectively by the data architecture. Finally, if new physical data environments are being introduced by the project, the existing technical architecture will have to be extended to fully support the new environment.

Design data environments

The content of each data environment should be designed in detail. Design requires a close knowledge of the performance characteristics of the data environment to ensure that the non-functional constraints imposed on the data can be met. For example, while a data model in Third Plus Normal Form is considered an adequate analysis model, the data implementation in a relational database will usually be partially de-normalized to meet the performance requirements. If a non-relational database is used, then the final implementation may bear little resemblance to the logical data model; see Figure 6.3.

In addition, capabilities such as the use of indices to support alternative entry points must be factored into the design, with the performance benefits and costs of each thoroughly assessed. The component-based development approach assists with this work by formalizing the access paths, which can then be optimized accordingly.

More complex still will be the consideration of *transaction management*. This will require an understanding of the likely volumes of different transactions and the scope of each. Scope will affect the number of data structures involved (e.g. the number of tables in a relational database), the amount, duration and granularity of data locking, and the use of commit and rollback, including in a multi-environment situation the use and semantics of multi-phase commits.

In a new physical data environment, these design factors can be considered in relative isolation. Where the physical data environment already exists, many of the design decisions will already have been taken; the new solutions will have to live with them. Only in circumstances of a very high-priority solution with demanding performance targets would change normally be considered, given the potential impact on existing IT systems and the costs of change.

When the data schema has been designed, test planning can begin. This plan will define the various tests that need to be performed, e.g. integrity tests, volume tests, loading tests. Much of this can be covered during data migration.

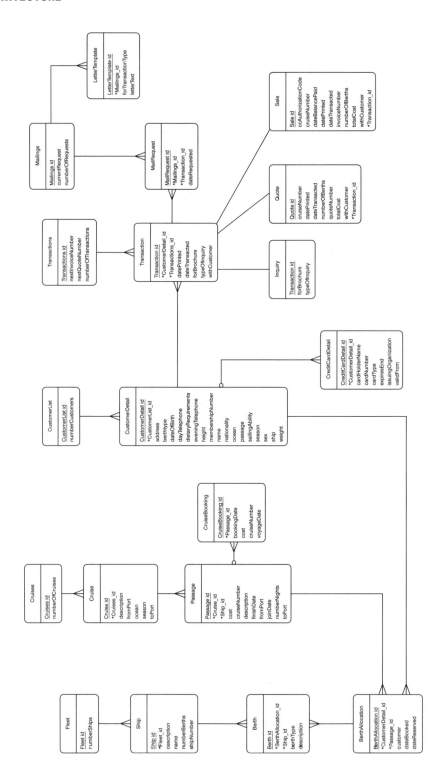

Figure 6.3
Example of a logical schema

Data migration planning

If data are to be migrated to new physical data environments, then the migration must be prepared carefully as losing information is expensive, if not fatal. As discussed in solution rollout (Chapter 5), the decision on big bang versus incremental migration has an impact on the whole rollout planning exercise.

While big-bang migration may either succeed or fail, the planning problem is focused on scheduling time to migrate the large volumes of data, during which time current operations must not be disrupted. However, incremental migration provides the opportunity to manage risk effectively, as it allows more flexibility in the rollout of the new solutions.

For incremental migration, the structures of the legacy and new data environments are compared to gain a clear understanding of the transformations that must be applied to the existing data in order to populate the new structures. A migration plan is created showing the patterns of migration and the order in which the procedures will be executed. Testing will reveal timing and performance information covering the migration, which is used to estimate the duration of the migration process. The migration (increment) can occur only when there is a sufficient window in the organization's operation to allow the process to be executed in its entirety.

The migration plan must also include a fallback position should the procedures fail on significant volumes of data, or duration of the exercise become greatly extended. At some stage in the process there will be a 'point of no return', when restoring the original position would (probably) take longer than completing the migration. Contingency planning must cover situations where significant problems are encountered after the point of no return.

Data store construction and rollout

The artifacts required to construct the data stores are assembled; these may include SQL, DDL scripts, XML schemata, and so on. The migration procedures and migration algorithms are designed, built, and tested to ensure that they operate correctly. This process is iterative, since the design of the procedures will be refined as additional data transformation cases are discovered. Procedures may have to be radically changed if they are unable to provide sufficient performance to complete the migration in a reasonable timescale.

As the new data stores are populated with the transformed test data, their performance can be evaluated against the non-functional requirements imposed. If the performance is unsatisfactory, the design must be changed, which will impact the migration procedures and the design of the data services that give access to the data.

Constructed data stores are made available in the testing environment and will be subject to configuration management procedures. This allows integrated solution builds to be tested through all the layers of the architecture. Faults found during solution testing, including both functional and non-functional faults, may result in changes being made to the new data stores, migration procedures and data services. Rollout of the new data architecture must be synchronized with the rollout of the new solutions and changes to legacy applications that require access to the new architecture. A key part of the rollout process will be the migration of data to the new architecture. The migration may make the rollout a lengthy process during which access to operational systems will have to be prevented.

Summary

Data architecture delivery ensures that the organization's informational needs are met in an effective and efficient manner. Organizations deal with information in different ways and at different levels and scales of working: component, solution, and organization. At the component level, specific databases may be provided to meet the needs of that individual component. When there are many components in a solution, then a cohesive data architecture and databases are needed to support the different components' information requirements. Finally, when the solution is to be integrated with other solutions, then the combined requirements of the data architectures and databases means that organizational level has been reached.

In all cases, the presence of existing data schemata and databases may place constraints and restrictions on the design of data architecture and services. Data migration planning then become necessary to ensure that the new solutions maintain information integrity and reliability.

Project management   7

Project management and planning provide the framework for the execution of each of the increments of development delivery: first, they enable the project to take place, start the increments, and monitor the project progress (see Figure 7.1). Should problems occur, then the enabling activity is revisited to adjust the process, the increments, and/or the resources. This pattern is repeated for each project and in fact is a pattern for all development activities; it is like a fractal pattern repeated at every level of activity: *enable, do, monitor.*

Software project management is a complex[1] job: every project is different, every team is different, stakeholders have different ideas, requirements change, time and budgets alter, etc. All these things add up to making life stressful for any project manager. None of these environmental variables is changed by the use of Select Perspective – they are inherent in the nature of project-based working.

However, Select Perspective has a number of features that address the issues that frequently arise in projects; these features include:

- use case driven
- iterative working
- incremental working
- parallel working
- active support for different project types.

1. Someone likened it to spinning plates.

Figure 7.1
Overview of project
management

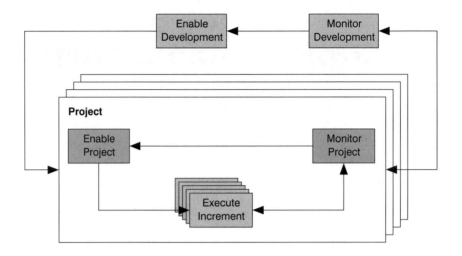

Use case driven

Use cases define the functional requirements for the solution. These are used to prioritize the order in which the increments are delivered. Priorities are set by the stakeholders in negotiation with the development teams; negotiation is key, as a simplistic statement such as 'all of it' does not define a useful goal.[2] Based on the priority of the use cases, it becomes possible to plan the order of project delivery. Use cases, encourage the iterative and incremental development approach and facilitate the management of change.

Iterative working

Iterations allow projects to meet changing requirements by modifying or adjusting remaining activities and deliverables as necessary. Designs and decisions are actively and frequently revisited as knowledge is gained through the execution of the project. Models are kept aligned as changes made in one view are used to update, refine, and refactor other views. Iteration need not be planned explicitly. For example, the task of modeling the services required by a use case includes the need to potentially change the use case based on knowledge gained by modeling the interaction. Iterations that manage changing requirements cannot be planned in advance; by definition, nothing is known about the change until it occurs. By planning in an iterative manner, however, change can be factored into plans even as they are being executed.

---

2. In any case, priorities will change during the project.

Incremental working

Increments deliver functioning and tested slices of the solution, which are treated as project milestones. The items delivered by each increment are determined from the priorities set for the project. Priorities must take account of the business need and the management of technical risk in the project. Increments are time-boxed in the project, and prioritization ensures that only low-priority items remain undelivered at the end of the project.

The result of this approach is that a working solution, sufficient to meet the urgent needs of the users, can be delivered earlier, e.g. launch with 100 percent of 86 percent of solution.

Parallel working

Besides iterations and increments, activities within the workflows of Select Perspective are executed simultaneously. With the supply–manage–consume approach to development, the workflows carefully separate the different concerns of the total development life cycle and may, therefore, be performed in parallel. However, there remains a natural ordering of activity: deliverables of one activity are prerequisites to others. These act as links between many of the activities within the parallel workflows; these links form a chain of outputs and inputs between the activities. For example, the use case model produced by the business alignment team is needed before the business architecture team can start.[3]

As project manager, it is possible to choose how the different workflows are balanced together in each increment in order to ensure the objectives of the increment are met.

Project types

Every project is different: the type of system that has to be delivered, the technology required, the size of the project, or the project's importance. Every project manager knows that one development approach will not fit all projects but must be tailored to match the characteristics of that project. Select Perspective acknowledges these differences by providing predefined 'process patterns' that help the project manager to define a specific way of working that fits the project. Select Perspective caters for many kinds of project types, including greenfield CBD, web-driven development, and package integration.

Web-driven development delivers a solution for the different styles of web-driven project:

- *e-information* describes those solutions that simply present content to the readers in basic HTML format;

3. This team could start after the first draft use case model so that they can acquaint themselves with the domain.

- *e-business* (B2B) covers those solutions where businesses perform supply-chain activities using web-based services; transactions are normally with trusted partners;
- *e-commerce* (B2C) describes transactions with consumers, when the interactions can be unpredictable and possibly insecure.

This style of development has a new workflow for *web content delivery*. This is often done in parallel with the main *web solution delivery* in order to launch the company's web presence (often called 'real estate' by the marketplace and web community). Web solution delivery designs, constructs, tests, and deploys a complete web-based solution using a web environment and runtime platform such as IBM Websphere.

Packages, that is enterprise-scale, off-the-shelf products such as enterprise resource planning or customer relationship management products, can be integrated in a similar way to legacy applications. Both need interfaces to be provided between the package and the system in development. Such facilities are provided through the Select Perspective approach to wrapping application functionality.

Different process patterns are defined to make Select Perspective fit for both small and larger projects, varying team sizes, or for business-critical projects and projects that deliver a system for a small group of users or one that has a short lifespan. In these cases, the project manager can choose a 'heavier' or 'lighter' approach, or anything 'in between'.

Increment planning

Before planning the next increment (Figure 7.2), a review of the progress, experiences, and issues needs to take place. Using this information, together with knowledge of the overall project objectives and priorities, the increment's objectives, can be defined. From these objectives, the deliverables in terms of scope and *state* are defined for the coming *increment*. Now that the deliverables have been defined, the tasks to create them can be identified and the amount of effort estimated. Tasks and resource allocations can now be planned in detail.

Figure 7.2
Overview of
increment planning

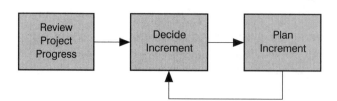

Review project progress

At the core of incremental working is the ability to respond rapidly and flexibly to changes in the status of the project. Status changes may be triggered by external influences such as changes in scope, timing, or resources, or by internal activity such as changing project velocity.[4] Working in increments allows the project to take these influences into account. In turn, this allows the project manager to respond quickly and effectively to the changing project circumstances by accurately setting the expectations of the project stakeholders and requesting changes in resources, timescales, or budget.

The end of an increment represents an important milestone for the project. It is good practice to organize a comprehensive *project review* involving the entire team, as this helps the team to achieve a sense of closure, and to assess the achievements and problems of the increment. Crucial to this closure is to gain an understanding of what has been achieved, and which deliverables remain incomplete. Also vitally important is identification of the issues and lessons that have been learned during the increment.

Information gathered in the increment review influences the decisions made about the scope of the next increment. Delivery metrics from the earlier increments are used to adjust the estimates assigned to tasks in the next increment.

Decide increment scope

The scope of the increment is achieved by considering the priorities of each of the requirements; these are used to establish the *objectives* of the increment. Each objective will require the creation of one or more deliverables. The tasks to be planned are those that will transform the current products into the deliverables specified for the coming increment.

Prioritization is based on use cases, as they provide the ideal planning medium for prioritizing requirements. First, there are the use cases that provide *value* to the business; these are sorted using MoSCoW[5] rules. Then the developers sort the use cases according to *risk*. In this case, risk refers to three levels: 'know how to implement'; 'know pretty much how to implement'; and 'no idea'. If everything ends up in the high-value pile with high risk, then you're in trouble! But normally there are trade-offs between business and developers, giving a sensible delivery schedule.

Once the use cases have been prioritized, then it is possible to prioritize the set of component services that now need to be developed on each business component to meet the requirements for the next set of use cases. This provides another form of MoSCoW rules for each component developer.

---

4. Project velocity is defined as the ratio between development effort and calendar time, e.g. 65 percent indicates a typical development velocity allowing for meetings, holidays, etc.
5. MoSCoW stands for 'must have', 'should have', 'could have', and 'won't have'. This gives 'weight' to each of the requirements.

Set increment objectives

The project team reviews the priorities assigned to the requirements. While the deliverables carried over from the previous increment will normally have the highest priority in the next increment, changes external to the project or specific project issues may act to change the priorities. Having understood the priorities, the objectives can be set for the increment. These are derived from the objectives of the project as a whole and the priorities set for the requirements.

Choose increment products

Each objective set for the increment helps to define one or more products that must be created by the increment. Product-based planning is a proven technique espoused by project management methods such as PRINCE 2.[6] When executing a project in an incremental manner, however, some products may be too large to complete in a single increment. To overcome this constraint, each product is defined in terms of its scope and state when delivered. For example, the project manager can define the use case model as a deliverable for an increment. For the full scope of the project, the state is to be 'use cases identified'; a smaller group of use cases is to be delivered in state 'use cases documented'; a (quantified) subset of this group is to be in the state 'use cases designed'.

Select increment tasks

The project manager understands the products that have been created so far (with their scope and state), and has chosen the products to be created by the coming increment. Tasks can be selected from the process definition that, taking the existing products as inputs, will create the selected products as their output. These tasks form the basis of the project plan for the increment. Creation of intermediate products defines the pattern of task dependencies within the plan. A process management tool such as Select Process Director (see Chapter 11) can assist in the creation of project-focused processes identifying the tasks that must be included in the project plan and the process-based dependencies that exist between them. Select Process Director can use this information to create or update a project plan, using project metric information gathered on previous projects and increments.

Update project plan

Identified tasks should be added to the project plan, together with the dependencies that exist between them. Effort estimates are attached to each task, together with resources assigned from the project team. At this point, the pro-

---

6. PRINCE 2 – 'Projects IN Controlled Environments' – is a project management methodology from the Central Computer and Telecommunications Agency (CCTA) of the UK government, developed from 1989 to 1996.

ject manager can take a reality check: can the objectives identified for the increment be fulfilled given the duration of the increment and the resources available? If resources are overloaded, then the project manager should adjust the plan to improve the balancing.

Hugely overloaded resources are a clear indication that the objectives being set for the increment are too ambitious. An option is to revisit the choices made in setting the scope of the increment. Some of the objectives can be removed from the scope of the increment, together with their deliverables and tasks. Project plans help to guide this process by indicating the scale of overloading and the effort involved in creating each deliverable. The project manager must also take into account the sequencing of the various deliverables when choosing which items will be removed from the scope. A deliverable that is a prerequisite for all the other deliverables selected for the increment cannot be taken out of the scope. Prioritization of objectives will provide the best guide to the sequence in which deliverables are removed from the scope; this information combined with the effort saving in each deliverable will indicate the items to be removed.

Summary

Project management and planning support the execution of each of the increments of development delivery. Before the increment can start, the objectives, resources, plans, etc. need to be agreed; this is the enabling phase. During the execution phase of the increment, the work is undertaken and progress against the plan is tracked. Should problems occur, then the enabling activity is revisited to adjust the process, the increments, and/or the resources.

The main deliverables from this workflow are:

- project plan
- risk register
- project statistics and metrics.

Roles 8

There are many roles involved in a project, many of which are common to all types of software development project. Each role is a set of responsibilities – not a job title – shared by one or more persons involved in the project, e.g. stakeholders, developers, managers.

This chapter focuses on those roles that are special to the contemporary development approach as well as those common roles where new skills are needed. Table 8.1 shows where each of the roles gets involved in the major workflows and their responsibilities.

Business architect

Understands and models the business activities of the organization, so projects can be aligned to a clearly understood set of business processes. Understands the business solutions that are available to the organization and how these act to support business processes.

Has sufficient experience to be able to undertake, manage and control significant business change projects. Is responsible for resolving conflicts between existing business architecture and the to-be solutions and for ensuring coordination between business change projects and related CBD projects.

Business architect authority

Understands models of the business activities of the organization and is responsible for ensuring that new models produced by projects adhere to the overall architecture of the organization. Arbitrates to resolve business architecture issues that exist between projects.

Table 8.1 Responsibilities for roles in the major workflows

Roles	Supply	Manage		Consume					
	Component Delivery	Manage	Business alignment	Business architecture	Technical architecture	Solution delivery	Solution rollout	Maintain and support	Data architecture
Business architect	I	I	P	I R	I	I	—	—	I
Business architect authority	I	P	C	C S	•I	I	—	—	I
Commercial/legal negotiator	C	I	A	—	A	—	A	—	—
Component architect	P C	—	A	A	—	A	—	—	I
Component developer	P	I	—	A	P	P	—	—	—
Data architect	I	—	—	—	—	—	—	—	P S
Data services developer	P	—	A	A	P	P	—	—	A R
Deployer	A	—	—	—	A	P	P	A	I
Deployment architect	C	—	—	—	C	C R	A R	—	I
Reuse administrator		P	—	—	—	—	—		
Reuse advisor	P	A	P	P	P	A	A	—	A
Reuse evaluator	A	P	—	—	—	—	—	—	—
Reuse librarian	I	P	—	—	—	—	—	—	—
Reuse manager	—	P	—	—	—	—	—	—	—
Solution developer	—	—	A	A	—	P	A	A	A
Technical architect	A	—	A	A	P	A	—	A	—
Technical architect authority	C	—	C	C	P S	C	—	—	—
Technical architect specialist	I	—	—	—	P	A	—	—	—
Technical component developer	P	—	A	A	A	A	—	—	—
Test authority	P R	R	P R	P R	P R	P R	P R	R	P R

Key: *A = Assist, C = Coach/advise, I = Provide Information, P = Perform, R = Review, S = Sign-off*

Commercial/legal negotiator

Negotiates the acquisition of components or services from commercial suppliers. Handles commercial and legal terms, service-level agreements, maintenance contracts, etc.

Component architect

Understands the architecture within which business or technical components are to be delivered, and the overall business information architecture that the components are servicing. Ensures that components adhere to the architectures as they are constructed and modified so that alignment to the business requirement is maintained.

Component developer

Understands and models the structure and behavior within a particular component ('inside the box'), whether this involves understanding of legacy or new technology. The role player will normally be skilled in the design of components and have the appropriate programming skills to construct them. Is responsible for delivering components, writing test cases from the design specifications for the code of component services, for testing the code of component services, and for resolving findings during black-box testing.

Data architect/database administrators

Understands and models the data used by the organization so that the data managed by business solutions will meet the requirements of the organization. Understands the business solutions that are available within the organization and how these structure and manage their information. Has sufficient experience to be able to undertake, manage, and control databases. Is responsible for resolving conflicts between existing data architectures and those required by new business solutions.

Data services developer

Understands and models the use of data for specific business or technical services in a particular environment. The role player will normally be skilled in the design of databases and data services and have the appropriate programming skills to construct data services. Is responsible for developing the data service component, writing test cases from the design specifications for the code of data services, for testing the code of data services and for resolving findings during black-box testing.

Deployer

The deployer is responsible for implementing the deployment of components and software parts (e.g. server pages, graphics) to the physical deployment nodes (servers). This includes following the deployment standards and procedures, maintaining the deployment models and documentation and support for the solution delivery, component delivery and technical architecture delivery teams.

Deployment architect

Responsible for setting, maintaining and evangelizing the deployment architecture for an enterprise. This includes managing the skills transfer and activities of the deployers within the operations team, and the creation and maintenance of the deployment architecture documentation and standards. Additionally, quality assurance and training support are provided to the deployer and the architects in the solution, component and technical architecture delivery teams.

Reuse administrator

Responsible for identifying strategic requirements, planning the acquisition of software assets, and monitoring contracts with suppliers, and for negotiations with the internal teams on their reuse levels within designs and implementations.

Reuse advisor

Responsible for maximizing the achieved levels of software reuse within the organization: first, by helping business solution teams to take advantage of opportunities for reuse (sowing); and second, by ensuring that potentially reusable resources are correctly modeled, cataloged and published for reuse by other teams (harvesting).

The reuse advisor has a good working knowledge of existing systems, packages, databases, generic models, and available components. This knowledge is used to assess reuse opportunities (for example, legacy systems and local models) and to evaluate reuse requirements. The role identifies areas for reuse improvement and pollinates reuse across solution projects.

Reuse evaluator

Responsible for identifying, assessing, examining, testing, and certifying external software assets that may be reused within the organization.

Reuse librarian

Ensures that components meet certification guidelines, classifies and stores components and services in the repository, and maintains the integrity of that asset repository.

Reuse manager

The reuse manager plans and controls the activities of the component and service team, makes policy decisions concerning reuse, and monitors component projects. Also sets guidelines for certification and classification, and ensures that assets meet the corporate goals. Acts as a 'champion' of reuse.

Solution developer

Models and interprets user requirements, using a range of skills and techniques to develop the models through to the implementation of effective solutions. These players will normally be skilled in the design of user interfaces and have the appropriate programming skills to construct the user interfaces and/or controllers. Creates a complete solution by controlling the interactions between components. Is responsible for writing test cases from the design specifications for the code of solution behavior, for testing that code and for resolving findings during black-box testing. Each project will involve several solution developers, each with different levels of knowledge, skills and experience.

Technical architect

Ensures that the technical architecture is correct and consistent with standards. Selects the delivery vehicle that fits the requirements. Different architects will be responsible for different delivery vehicles. Is responsible for the creation of the proper delivery vehicles.

Technical architecture authority

Sets the technical standards and controls configuration management procedures. The role ensures technical coherence and consistency across different teams.

Technical architecture specialist

Understands and models the technical environment, which includes hardware platforms, networks, databases, and the web, in a way that projects can be undertaken in the context of a clearly defined technical environment. Understands the fit of all hardware, networks, and databases that are available to the organization and how these act to support the technical process. Is responsible for specific areas of technology.

Technical component developer

Responsible for the construction of components and other assets that will form part of the technical architecture for a specific delivery vehicle.

Test authority

Responsible for the oversight of testing activity for projects. Takes responsibility for the creation and documentation of testing strategies, techniques and processes. Is ultimately responsible for ensuring that projects undertake sufficient testing during their execution and that the testing is performed at appropriate times, using appropriate techniques and resources.

Summary

Each person involved in the project, whether a stakeholder, a developer, or a manager, has an opportunity to extend their responsibilities and skills with roles that are special to the contemporary development approach as well as those common roles where new skills are needed.

Techniques   9

Various techniques are used in Select Perspective, many of which are common to all types of software development project. This chapter focuses on those techniques that are special to the component and service development approach as well as those common ones where new skills are needed. Every project does not need all the techniques outlined here. For agile development, a minimal set of techniques would be applied, but for a major enterprise-scale development many more techniques would be used.

Table 9.1 shows where each of the techniques is mainly used in the major workflows. Examples of the deliverables for many of the listed techniques can be found in the appended case study.

Business component identification

Business components can be identified in a number of ways: brainstorming, textual analysis, or use case analysis. Usually, combinations of these approaches are used to provide the first-cut model of the business components. This combination of ways is called 'chunking' and is usually undertaken as a joint session involving users and analysts.

A basic approach is:

1 Brainstorm a list of nouns or business services that describe the system (see strategies below.)

2 Group those nouns into a maximum of seven groups; there is no optimum number of chunks, but the number should be kept small and focused.

3 Review that grouping and add or reduce the number as appropriate.

Table 9.1 Main use of technique in a workflow

Workflows	Supply	Manage			Consume				
Technique	Component delivery	Manage	Business alignment	Business architecture	Technical architecture	Solution delivery	Solution rollout	Maintain and support	Data architecture
Business component identification				✓					
Component design	✓			✓	✓	✓			
Component interaction modeling	✓			✓	✓	✓		✓	✓
Component interface design	✓			✓	✓	✓		✓	
Component modeling	✓			✓	✓	✓		✓	
Design by contract	✓			✓	✓	✓			
Gap analysis	✓	✓	✓	✓	✓	✓	✓	✓	✓
Incremental development	✓		✓	✓	✓		✓		✓
Package modeling	✓			✓					
Refactoring	✓	✓	✓	✓	✓	✓	✓	✓	✓
Reuse	✓	✓	✓	✓	✓	✓	✓	✓	✓
Test case specification from a process thread diagram			✓	✓	✓				
Test case specification from a use case	✓			✓		✓			
Test case specification from an interaction diagram	✓				✓	✓			
Thin-slice prototyping	✓			✓	✓	✓	✓	✓	✓
Use case modeling		✓	✓	✓	✓	✓	✓	✓	
Use of patterns	✓			✓	✓	✓	✓	✓	✓

There are two strategies for discovering components: *business semantics-driven* and *service-driven*. A balanced approach works best, as excessive reliance on either approach leads to a distorted model.

The business semantics-driven approach centers on looking for concepts in the business that fulfill the definition of a component. The focus is on *nouns*, particularly singular collective nouns, in a business requirements statement, rather than verbs.

A service-driven approach centers on asking what business *services* are required of the system. Candidate components provide cohesive sets of services with minimal interfaces. The approach is often used in conjunction with class–responsibility–collaboration cards (CRC cards) [Beck and Cunningham].

Both these techniques can be applied to a variety of source material, such as the use cases.

Component design

Component design refers to the design of the internal parts of a component. As a component encapsulates its internal structure, different design techniques may be required: object-oriented approach, structured methods, database scripting, etc. There are a number of ways to design components, depending on the intended content:

- To encapsulate the functionality/data of heritage systems: design a *wrapper*.
- Reuse of another component that provides some of the required functionality: design an *adaptor*.
- To integrate a software package: design a *wrapper* or an *adaptor*.
- New development: design an *object-oriented* solution.

A *wrapper*, as its name implies, wraps up the functionality of an existing system by providing a router to the system interface. For example, in the scenario of authorizing a credit card using an existing banking authorization service, a component provides the interface to convert authorization messages into appropriate API calls to the authorization system. An *adaptor* not only encapsulates existing functionality, for example as a wrapper or with respect to another component, it also provides extra features. This is useful when, say, a component from a third-party supplier does not provide the exact set of services for the solution, so extra classes are added to meet the requirements.

The component supply team also needs to define the *principles of the design*: is it to be highly flexible, maintainable, high-performance, or what percentages of the three? To establish this, the team needs to verify the component responsibilities and participation in use cases against the non-functional requirements for the application and assess the stability of the requirement, and the business's future requirements for change.

To *model the design*, consider the component as a micro-system where the interface services are the use cases. Therefore, provide a sequence diagram showing the interaction of the parts (classes, external components, etc.) to meet the needs of each service. Consider how error handling and recovery will be executed, component instantiation e.g. lazy instantiation (only load when you need the object), transaction management, memory management, etc. Many of these facilities are provided by *technical components,* and the *technical architecture patterns.*

Component interaction modeling

This is a use of *interaction modeling* involving only the interfaces to components. The components are treated as 'black boxes' whose implementation detail is hidden away. Component interaction modeling is used to explore the services that must be offered by components in order to fulfill the functional requirements of a business solution described by its use cases. The services identified may already exist, in which case they will be reused by the business solution being modeled, while other services will be new.

Component interaction modeling takes place on a per use case basis. An interaction diagram (UML sequence or collaboration diagram) is associated with the use case. The only objects represented on the interaction diagram are the interfaces to the components that are involved in the interaction. Each message sent to an object on the diagram represents the invocation of a service that must be offered by the component receiving the message.

Most component interactions will use the fork pattern, so most service requests originate from the system boundary or actor. This avoids the inter-component invocation of services and results in far fewer dependencies between components being created.

Component interface design

Design of the component interface goes through a number of stages: identification of the component responsibilities, negotiation of the derived services, and specification of the services (operations and signatures).

An interface is a *stereotype* of a class. Interfaces offer services to clients that express the responsibilities of the interface. When specifying interfaces, you may also define interface attributes that relate to the underlying information model of the package. It is important to understand the difference between an interface specification and implementation. When specifying an interface, we capture the *contract* between a client and the services offered by the interface. This may involve the specification of state changes resulting from service invocation expressed by changes in interface attribute values.

Component modeling

This provides a blueprint of all the different aspects of the component. Like any blueprint it has a number of viewpoints: the interface, the internal structure of parts, and the interaction between the parts. These viewpoints are presented as a set of UML diagrams that together define the model of the component.

Component modeling involves a number of different techniques that are suitable for the various viewpoints of the component:

- *the interface*: component interface design;
- the internal structure of parts: object-oriented analysis and design; class modeling; use of patterns;
- the interaction between the parts: interaction modeling; state modeling; use of patterns.

Component testing

As a component is a well-bounded (encapsulated) collection of parts, it can be treated as a subsystem for testing. This means that each part needs to be tested (unit test), then the interaction between the parts (system test), and finally the component services themselves (user test). Testing is driven by the test *specification* for the component.

When a component consists of classes, each class instance (object) must be tested individually. This is normally done through exercising their operations via a *test harness*. Once you are confident in the operations of the individual classes, they can be tested working with other class instances as identified on the interaction diagrams for the component. Test cases can be derived from the interaction diagrams produced for each interface service.

Final user testing, where the user is another client component, ensures the quality of all component parts. Test cases are derived from both component interaction diagrams and use cases.

Deployment modeling

The UML modeling of deployment of software component to physical nodes, e.g. web pages on web servers. *The deployment model* represents the planned and actual location and relationships between the runtime parts of the solution, i.e. the components.

In UML, this is presented as a *deployment diagram*, which is a static structure of the nodes and their connections. From the UML specification a deployment diagram is defined as:

> a graph of nodes connected by communication associations. A node represents a runtime computational resource, which generally has at least a memory and often computational capability. Nodes may contain component instances. This indicates that the component lives or runs on the node and as the component may contain objects it also indicates that the objects reside on that node.
>
> [OMG-UML V1.3]

Any deployment diagram created when planning the deployment does not show the *actual* relationships unless the deployer physically maintains and updates the diagram.

In Select Component Manager, it is possible to show the planned and the actual deployment. This is presented as a *deployment tree* diagram showing the nodes and under each node the list of deployed components and a list of associated nodes, i.e. the dependencies. This deployment tree diagram can be created by dragging and dropping components into nodes. After the physical deployment has taken place and any adjustments or changes have been made to the operational environment, e.g. new components added, updates to the runtime support such as IBM Websphere, then these can be synchronized with the original deployment tree to show the actual deployment. It is also possible to synchronize with an empty tree to get the existing deployed components into Select Component Manager. This means that the structure and dependencies of the components in any unknown operational environment or node can be determined.

Design by contract

Design by contract [Meyer] describes the responsibilities of the calling and called components, by describing the preconditions, post-conditions, and parameters for each service invocation. This is the most important aspect of documenting a component, so that it can be easily used and reused.

Preconditions express the constraints for a service to operate properly, and the post-conditions express the state of the component after the service has been invoked successfully. This then defines the benefits and obligations for the supplier and consumer of the service: the contract. If the obligations are not fulfiled, then the contract has been broken.

During design of a component or service, the preconditions and post-conditions of the service are fully defined and agreed. This is critical, as unless these conditions are documented any defect will spread through the solutions.

The caller of a service must always check the preconditions and take care of error handling, based upon those checks. The invoked service will never check the preconditions, otherwise duplicate checks and error-handling mechanisms will be implemented. The invoked service of the called component must always deliver the required post-conditions, unless a technical exception occurs. Technical exceptions may include the temporary unavailability of database or network resources. The calling components should check these exceptions after the service has been invoked and before attempting to use the result of the service invoked.

Like any contract, the benefits of a guaranteed outcome from the invoked service places obligations on the user of that service. Ignore the contract and the results are unpredictable and possibly disastrous. Also, as there is a contract, any code that verifies that preconditions have been met is unnecessary, as is any code to verify that the service operated correctly. The obligations for each contractual party are clear.

Gap analysis

Gap analysis is the comparison between two forms of similar deliverables, such as designs, models, components, services, and subsystems, to identify areas of difference and overlap. By undertaking gap analysis early and frequently in the project's life cycle to many of the deliverables, many opportunities for reuse can be found. For example, a design may be similar to the one planned, and all that is needed is for the extra features to be added.

Gap analysis is most commonly used in comparing a component's requirements with published components in the component repository as part of the provisioning phase in the consume workflow. Even if there is no exact match, the work to fill the gap may be straightforward, with the benefit of reusing existing and proven services. Gap analysis is also used when designing by contract; can you meet the preconditions? are the post-conditions fulfilled to your requirements? Unless these are in alignment, you have a gap.

Incremental development

The execution of a software development project is in a series of increments, so that deliverables are created in a controlled, phased manner and 'big-bang' impacts are avoided. Incremental development is one of the key cornerstones of Select Perspective. The execution of a project is undertaken as a series of increments, each typically of six to ten weeks duration.

The project itself has its own objectives that it must fulfill; these act to define how the project will be delivered. From the project objectives, more specific objectives can be defined for each increment. Work within the increment is planned so as to fulfill the objectives by creating the required deliverables. The objectives and deliverables for each increment are different; consequently, the application of the workflows and the workflow activities undertaken will be different.

Increments are restricted to being completed within a planned time box. Work outstanding when the time box is completed must be replanned for completion in a later increment (often the following increment.) At the end of each increment, the outcome of the increment is assessed against the objectives set. The outcome will have an impact on the planning of the forthcoming increment, not only in terms of what work has to be done but also in terms of adjusting the metrics applied to the plan.

In component-based development, incremental working is greatly facilitated by use cases. Use cases not only represent an effective way of documenting the external, behavioral functionality of the required solution, they also serve as convenient 'units of work' for the planning, control, execution, and monitoring of the project.

The creation of models with high levels of traceability allows the activities needed to produce the planned deliverables for an increment to be predicted and planned with a high degree of accuracy. Effective project planning and management is greatly facilitated by these high levels of traceability.

Package modeling

This is modeling the relationships between packages where a package has two distinct forms: as a representation of a component, or as a set of services implemented on part of the runtime system architecture, i.e. a node.

The UML package symbol is used to represent a component during modeling activities as it represents the encapsulation of parts that offer an «interface» to other components. During modeling, it is critical to identify the *dependencies* between all components. This is shown on a class diagram with component (package) symbols and dependent associations.

Once a component is allocated to a node shown on a *deployment* diagram, then this UML package symbol represents the collection of services provided by all components on this node. It is an implementation view of the packages.

Refactoring

Refactoring is reorganizing the structure of an existing component or solution to make it easier to understand and cheaper to modify without changing its observable behavior.

> Refactoring is the process of changing a software system in such a way that it does not alter the external behavior of the code yet improves its internal structure. It is a disciplined way to clean up code that minimizes the chances of introducing defects. In essence when you refactor you are improving the design of code after it has been written.
>
> [Fowler]

Refactoring is a common activity as the project develops. Components need to be refactored to provide a better interface, and parts of components need to be restructured to meet new service requirements. One such cause of refactoring is when the developers detect a 'bad smell'[1] coming from the code: the code is clumsy, awkward, or complex.

These are some examples of different ways to overcome code that has a 'bad smell':

- *Long parameter list*: replace parameter with method, or introduce parameter object.
- *Long message chain*: hide delegates.
- *Duplicated code*: extract method, extract class, or pull-up method.
- *Switch statements*: replace conditional with polymorphism, replace type code with subclasses, replace parameter with explicit methods.

Reuse

Reuse is the philosophy of finding suitable assets, whether models, diagrams, code fragments, or components, that can provide a starting solution.

Reuse is a fundamental philosophy of systems development that can be adopted across an organization if it is to achieve its potential in terms of

---

1. Kent Beck introduced this phrase to describe when to refactor, i.e. when certain structures in code suggest a poor design or careless modifications. Attributed to his grandmother, who said 'if it stinks, change it'.

shortening development project duration and reducing costs. Reuse is not constrained to business components or other software assets. Any of the intellectual capital of an organization that has been captured in a suitable form is available for reuse. Such assets include:

- development processes
- project plans
- project requirements
- analysis and design models
- test scripts
- test plans
- source code
- deployed executables.

To achieve success with a reuse philosophy, the following capabilities should be implemented to support reuse within an organization:

- *library*: to act as a repository of the reusable artifacts available;
- *search*: so that specific items can be found and reused;
- *standards*: so items are described consistently to facilitate searching;
- *management*: to ensure quality and encourage the adoption of the reuse culture;
- *sowing*: encouraging the reuse of assets by projects;
- *harvesting*: finding new items from projects that can be reused;
- *publishing*: dissemination of information about assets through the library.

Reused assets feature much higher quality than uniquely developed resources simply because of the levels of use to which they have already been subjected. However, all reuse programs must overcome the 'not invented here' syndrome: rejecting reuse because the items were implemented by others.

Test case specification from a process thread diagram

Specify the order in which tests should occur during integration and acceptance testing, based on sequencing information derived from *business process thread* and *use case* diagrams.

The process thread diagram describes the sequence in which elementary business processes (EBP) or activities are performed within an overall process. Many of the functional requirements for a business solution, expressed as use cases, will be derived from the EBPs. In consequence, the process thread diagram can be used to sequence the test cases to be performed during integration or acceptance testing. The use case diagram provides information about how use cases relate to each other with 'uses' and 'extends' relationships. This information supplements the sequencing information derived from the process thread.

Process thread diagrams show the sequence in which the main use cases should be tested. The use case diagram shows which related use cases need to be tested at specific points in the sequence.

In addition to this information, consideration must be given to the course tested in each use case, since the execution of a specific course will probably affect the related use cases that are executed. In some cases, the course executed will also affect the sequence of tests. In consequence, each process thread will form a test cluster with multiple sequence test cases associated with it.

Test case specification from a use case

The work in a CBD project is structured around the set of use cases that define the behavioral requirements of the business solutions. In particular, the incremental delivery of the use cases strongly favors the idea of testing being structured on the same basis. In this case, the test clusters and their test cases must be derived from the use cases too.

The test cluster will contain all the test cases related to a single use case. Each test case will test a course, either the basic or an alternative course, through the use case. Use case preconditions will apply to all the test cases in the test cluster, since the preconditions must be fulfilled in order for any of the courses to be executed at all. The use case preconditions become the test cluster preconditions.

The interactions between the user and the business solution in the use case course are used to describe the actions that will be performed in the use case. The author of the test case must specify suitable values to be entered, and the values that will be output following a specific interaction. These values may be the data retrieved from a test database or calculated by business rules in response to the values entered. If the business solution will also show specific responses (e.g. messages being displayed) before the final completion of the interaction, these must also be described.

Many courses will contain conditional behavior that is only invoked if specific conditions are fulfilled by the user during the interaction. Sufficient test cases must be created to test each item of conditionality and each permitted combination of conditions within each course.

The post-conditions of the use case describe what must be true in terms of the state of the business solution once the use case has been completed. Most post-conditions relate to the persistent data stored by the business solution. If the user cancels the interaction or is unable to complete the interaction because an error is generated as part of the test case, then the use case has not been completed. The post-conditions will not apply and the preconditions will still apply to the business solution. Test cases involving the cancellation of the interaction at different points in the dialog should also be created.

If the basic course has been constrained by additional pre- and post-conditions that serve to help to define the choices made by the user (helping to simplify the basic course), these can be used as constraints on the test cases of the various courses. The basic course can be tested by ensuring that the interaction fulfills the basic course preconditions.

Alternative courses can be tested by violating each combination of basic course pre- and post-conditions in turn. Each test case describes which basic course pre- and post-conditions are being violated and, if there is more than one potential violation, how the condition is being violated. The interaction describes the user's actions and the systems responses in the normal way.

Test case specification from an interaction diagram

White-box tests are prepared by using the interaction diagrams as abstract program scripts. Each interaction diagram shows how the classes, component interfaces, and other items of interest interact to provide the behavior described in the use case courses. Given the interaction diagram and a set of pre- and post-conditions to constrain the test, the precise pattern of interaction that should occur can be predicted and documented. When the code is executed, the pattern of code execution can be confirmed against the script provided.

Thin-slice prototyping

A thin-slice prototype provides confidence in the development process, the technology, the team skills, etc. by demonstrating a small amount of functionality, e.g. displays single customer account.

One of the principles of the thin-slice prototype is to get feedback, interpret it, and put what is learned back into the development as quickly as possible. This is true of the business users learning how best the system can contribute, and feeding back that learning in days or weeks instead of months or years. This is also true of developers learning how best to design, implement and test the system, and feeding back that learning in days, or weeks.

In the early days of the project, it is critical to gain the experience of the development process, the development environment, the technical architecture framework, and the target platform. By developing a thin-slice prototype, every area of the development (tools, technology, etc.) can be explored. This exposes both understanding and problem areas, which are best discovered early in the project.

Use case modeling

Use case modeling is one of the key techniques applied during CBD projects. Use cases are important because their relevance to the project extends beyond being part of the statement of requirements.

Use cases are crucial to:

- the organization of work is structured in the project;
- the planning, management and control of the project;
- the construction, testing and delivery of the software;
- the management of changes in requirements.

Each use case describes a way in which the system will be used to provide value to the actor. The use case takes the form of a dialog between the actor and the system. Use cases focus on describing the external behavior. Use cases do not define complex internal behavior such as the use of business rules or the algorithmic content of the requirements.

The use case model describes the scope of the business solution to be built by defining:

- *actors* – which are external;
- *use cases* – which are internal.

The semantics of the use case model are very simple. Each use case is associated with one or more actors, who will execute the use case. Use cases can also be associated with each other. Two forms of association exist:

- *uses* – where one use case always makes use of another;
- *extends* – where one use case may optionally make use of another.

Since actors are external to the system, their definition is not crucial to the ultimate success of the project. It is sufficient to name and briefly describe each actor. In contrast, the use cases are vital to the project. The key elements to be described for each use case are:

- *intent* – what the use case will be used to achieve;
- *description* – the way in which the use case will be most commonly executed;
- *preconditions* – that must be met before the use case can be invoked;
- *post-conditions* – that must be true when the use case is completed;
- *alternative courses* – other, less common, ways of completing the use case.

Note that the preconditions and post-conditions apply to the use case as a whole, i.e. they govern the basic course and all the alternative courses. It can be helpful to describe how the basic course is constrained (additional preconditions and post-conditions that must be true in order to make use of the basic course.) Doing this helps to verify the set of alternative courses for the use case, since each alternative course must be taken as a result of violating one or more of the preconditions or post-conditions that constrain the basic course.

During requirements identification, the use case model is deliberately kept very simple. It is usually sufficient to identify the alternative courses with a headline rather than describing them in detail. If the basic course is constrained by additional preconditions and post-conditions, the headline to each alternative course should indicate which condition is being violated. Some conditions can be violated in several ways, so the way in which a condition is violated should also be described. The use cases should not be decomposed with uses or extends associations. The use case model typically only shows each actor making use of a group of use cases.

During requirements analysis, the modeling of use cases is extended. The service invocations required to implement each use case are modeled using an interaction diagram. At this stage, the identification of patterns of service usage becomes possible – these patterns indicate reuse of the same pattern of services within a single use case or across multiple use cases (or both.) Based on this identified reuse, the use case model can be decomposed with uses and extends associations.

Functional decomposition of use cases should be avoided; use cases should be decomposed only on the basis of identified reuse. The description of the basic and alternative courses is not a sufficient basis for identifying reuse, although descriptions can be strongly indicative of reuse. Reuse is confined by finding patterns of service usage during requirements analysis. Only at this stage should the use cases be decomposed.

Use cases describe the interaction between the actor and the system, so they are excellent in situations where significant user interface activity is required to trigger the behavior of the system. Many systems also include significant batch activity, where the interaction required to trigger the activity is very small (or even non-existent for time-triggered activity.) In these cases, it can help to decompose the batch process into its functional parts by applying some functional decomposition. Each of the decomposed use cases is associated with another use case representing the entire batch process. It can be helpful to think of this larger use case as a form of actor. The description of each use case is phrased at a suitable level of abstraction: the batch process describes the broad steps of the whole process, while the decomposed use cases describe more detail for each step.

Use of patterns

Patterns are akin to recipes, and can be applied to many modeling problems. Each pattern is expressed in abstract terms, together with examples, which make its intent apparent.

The pattern is applied to the model by taking the elements of the pattern and reinterpreting them in the light of the modeling context. In the simplest cases, only more specific names need be given to the items in the pattern. More complex cases may require the structure of the pattern to be altered before it can be successfully applied to the model.

A more recent development in the patterns arena is the creation of *anti-patterns*. Patterns describe ideas that are beneficial, that will make a positive contribution to the project outcome. In contrast, anti-patterns describe ideas that are harmful and will be disruptive to the success of a project. The motive for the documentation of anti-patterns is to avoid the ideas and forms of behavior described.

Many large software vendors are beginning to focus on the concept of *frameworks*, which can be considered very large patterns. The framework supplies the concepts, models and, sometimes, structural elements of the code. Within this supplied framework, the organization can implement its own specific algorithmic behavior based on its processes and business activity.

Patterns can be obtained from many different public sources, including books, magazines, and internet websites. Patterns also manifest themselves in models that have already been created and simply need to be recognized and abstracted so that they can be used to speed the development of new models. One such example is Select Perspective Patterns, which provide a set of models and assets that can be used on many projects.

During *domain modeling*, patterns may be found in terms of business processes and the way in which important business concepts are managed. Since these patterns are predicated on the way the business operates, the requirements defined by previous projects may act as important sources of potential patterns. During *requirements identification*, simple patterns can be found in use case models, particularly with respect to the way use cases are decomposed, while during *requirements analysis*, patterns can be applied to all the models developed during analysis. Recent work has revealed the existence of simple but powerful patterns in business components; these patterns reflect not only the components that are found but also the dependencies they share and, in many cases, the major services that must be offered. Patterns also exist that describe how specific business situations can be modeled effectively within the analysis model. These are finer-grained patterns that will influence the way specific components are structured.

During *solution delivery*, the use of patterns was initially based around providing solutions for problems frequently encountered during the design process. In consequence, there is a very rich seam of patterns to be tapped at the design level.

Organizations often contribute to this pool of patterns by documenting at least some of their systems infrastructure as patterns rather than as generic infrastructure components. This technique is useful when there is a common structure to all the solutions to a frequently occurring problem, but within the common structure, widely varying algorithms must be used to meet specific requirements.

Summary

The preceding techniques provide a subset of the complete set of techniques and examples in the full version of Select Perspective.

Deliverables 10

Select Perspective is a delivery-based approach to contemporary software development. Other development approaches focus on activities and tasks that can lead to unnecessary work in producing deliverables that may have little value. In Select Perspective, the emphasis on deliverables means that only those deliverables of value to the project need to be produced; anything not on the delivery line can be avoided. For example, if the proposed solution is for a small part of a business process such as mailings, then the business process models need not be delivered.

This chapter organizes those important deliverables into each of the major workflows: supply, manage, and consume. Examples for each of the deliverables can be found in the complete version of Select Perspective, and many examples of diagrams such as use cases are to be found in the appended case study.

Supply

Supply involves reusing, renting, buying, and building components or services. The two major workflows for building components and services are *component delivery* and *technical architecture delivery*.

Component delivery

Component delivery covers the specification of the component services, designing the internal architecture in terms of its classes, and combining these with the technical architecture deliverables to deliver an executable package for the component. As well as the component itself, in its three different forms – business, data, and technical – there are different deliverables that reflect aspects of the component, e.g. its interface, or its test specification.

Component

A component is a unit of software that conforms to a component model and can be deployed and composed independently without modification according to a composition standard. Software entities interact with a component using the component's clearly defined interfaces; an interaction standard defines the elements of the interface. These are the characteristics of a component:

- Components are *units of deployment*, i.e. they run within computer systems. Simply designing components and not converting the design into run-able components adds little benefit to the final solution.
- Each component has a *published interface* that defines its responsibilities as a set of services, e.g. know about customer. There must be at least one interface to each component, but a component may have multiple interfaces that allow different views/access to the component or different communication mechanisms.
- *Communications standards* are important for components as they need to interact with other components to provide the necessary functionality.
- Components are *assembled to realize solutions*. Components themselves are constructed and tested as normal. When completed they are then combined with other new or reused components to form the system solution.

There are a number of different kinds of component: *business components, technical components,* and *data components*. Each has a similar related set of products: specification, interface, model, implementation, and executable and deployment.

The *component specification* defines the requirements, and scopes the deployment unit, for a component. *Interfaces* define a set of services that encapsulate functionality for the component. There may be several interfaces for each component. The component *model* that specifies the internal design of the component can be accessed through the component services; services have a name and a parameter list. *Implementation* (or source code) defines how services execute. Several implementations may be required, depending on the platforms or environments being targeted. There may be several *executables* for each implementation to support; for example, debug and release versions of software. *Deployment* defines the runtime dependencies of the component as well as their allocation to any available computational resource.

If the components are specified, designed, and constructed by your organization, then you would expect to see all these parts. However, if the component comes from a third-party supplier, then you may only receive the interface and executable parts.

The component's products are detailed in the following sections.

Component specification

The component specification defines the requirements for a component or service. This specification is used in the negotiation between the component suppliers and consumers. Once agreed, it forms a *supply contract* with the service provider or component implementer, solution assembler, and tester. A component specification defines the encapsulation boundary, i.e. the line between what is visible to the consumers and what is considered as internal, 'hidden' by the suppliers.

The component specification defines the requirements for a single component. It consists of:

- *required interface* defining of usage contract between the component and its clients, by means of the interface the component is required to present;
- *external dependencies* usually on services from other components or from external sources such as legacy systems, software packages or information feeds;
- *non-functional requirements* and constraints on the component, for example its scalability or a need to run on a certain operating system.

The level of detail contained in the component specification may vary according to the type of component and which stage the project has reached. Early in the project, components will be specified at a high level, with general descriptions of the interface, the design options, and the non-functional requirements. As the project progresses, such descriptions will be formalized such that towards the end of the project the component specification can act as a detailed contract for the services that the component provides.

A component specification may list several interfaces according to the environment in which the component is to be used and the services it is to provide. Each of these interfaces will require a unique description, as documented in the component interface.

Component interface

The component interface describes one or more sets of services provided by the component; these services express the responsibilities of the component

This interface describes the *external view of the component*. In the simplest terms, the interface lists the services provided by the component. That is, it specifies its services according to an interaction standard that defines how each service looks and how it is accessed. Good design practice dictates that access to the services provided by a component should require as little knowledge as possible of the component's internal workings (for example, the classes or the internal behavior of the component.) Hence a good component interface should provide as much as possible of the information necessary to use the services of the component.

This information includes, for each service:

- *Service signature*: the signature defines the form of the service, in terms of its name, its input parameters and any values it may return.

- *Service descriptions*: a service combines one or more operations to form a contract with users of that service. The types of service depend on the type of component, for example whether it is a technical component or a business component, or depending on the tier in which the component appears.

- *Exceptions*: the scope of the service, for example in terms of contextual state, resource availability or acceptable input parameters, and how the component will behave given such exception conditions.

It is common for this information to be published as part of the supply–manage–consume approach. Consumers examine existing component interfaces to find any that match their component specification. If no suitable interfaces are found, then the specification and a draft interface are published in order that suppliers (internal or external) may negotiate on the supply of those services. These services may be provided as a component or as a web service.

It is important to understand the difference between an interface specification and implementation. When specifying an interface, you capture the *service contract* between a client and the component in terms of the services offered by the interface. This may involve the specification of state changes resulting from service invocation expressed by changes in interface attribute values. The exact implementation of this specification will be based on design decisions and deployment constraints, neither of which should be of interest to the client.

Component model

The component model consists of a set of diagrams that describe a component from a number of viewpoints. These include definitions of the services provided by the component, the design of its internals, and definitions of its dynamic behavior. Key diagrams are class diagrams, object sequence diagrams, state diagrams, and a persistent data model. The diagrams in this model are used to communicate (in a common language/notation) the structure of the component.

The model is in effect a mini-solution, which follows the same design rules and constraints as any other project. The design may be undertaken by an individual or by a team. This component's designer or team may be part of the organization or an external supplier who knows only of the specification of the component services (see component specification).

The model itself consists of a set of UML diagrams. These include:

- A *use case diagram*, which shows each service as a use case.

- An *object sequence diagram* (OSD), which shows the interaction between the classes within the component for each service.

- The key diagram is the *class diagram*, showing the internal structure of the component parts, including interfaces, services classes, internal classes, external interfaces, and the relationships between them.

- Some of the component's classes may require *state diagrams*, which show the events and transitions to each new state. In a commercial system solution, these are not as common as in real-time system solutions, but they may be required for complex logic handling.

- The *data storage diagram* shows the structure of the entities and tables that support this component. This schema is combined with other component storage schemata in solution delivery.

The list above assumes that the component is constructed using object-oriented methods. When a component is a *wrapper* to another system such as mainframe-hosted logic, then the exact set of diagrams will differ. For example, there may be fewer classes in the class diagram, and the OSDs will show the mapping between component service requests and calls to the wrapped system.

The component model also contains documentation to support the diagrams described above. This includes a glossary, descriptions of the key artifacts, and a record of design decisions.

Component test specification

Test specifications are based on the component contracts specified by the pre-conditions, post-conditions and invariants (rules and constraints) on interface services. Test specifications also address the desired quality characteristics of the component.

The *component test specification* is one of the types of test specification defined in the *test strategy*. Each component requires a specification to define what needs to be tested and how testing should take place. It is important to test both the external (black box) view of the component, as viewed by other elements of the system, and the internal (white box) view, as viewed by the developers of the component.

The exact content of the component specification will depend on the type of component to be tested. The component test specification can cover:

- *Description*: a brief description of the component, and introductory information on how it should be tested (for example, a transaction component requires load testing, and a security component requires penetration testing.)

- *Test requirements*: a description of how the component is to be tested, including required hardware and software configurations, test setup procedures and locations of test data.

- *Interface tests*: a set of tests should exist for each service offered by the component. Each test should take the form of a service request of the component, and the resulting response should be checked against expected values and expected quality criteria. Negative testing, in which abnormal service requests are used, should also take place.

- *Internal tests*: testing of the internal workings of the component can take the form of code inspections, or unit testing of specific classes within the component.

● *Regression tests*: a selection of tests should be used to verify the consistency of the workings of the component over time. For these, it is especially important to specify where the test data and results are stored.

The test specification also defines the component test environment, for example any test harnesses or test tools. Test harnesses should be capable of executing a component both in isolation (with all dependencies stubbed out), and with selected dependent components in place.

It is important to ensure that tests cover the majority of code within a component. A combination of external and internal tests will be required to achieve a high level of test coverage. The component test specification references test cases to ensure that the majority of code is covered.

As some components may share testing procedures, for example all business components may require the same testing environment, such information can be documented separately and referenced from the component test specification.

Business component

A *business component* is a kind of component that provides services to support the business solution. This means that it encapsulates the required behavior and information to support business operations. Business components give the solution framework to the business users and enforce any business rules that affect the information, e.g. number of valid customer agreements.

Contained within a component are classes that are closely related, i.e. they form a cohesive group. Generally, the classes would all have the same lifetime, i.e. be created together and destroyed together. For example, a customer component may have classes for the company, billing address, delivery address, order history, credit limits, discount rules, and banking details.

Business components are designed to be highly flexible, i.e. any changes are contained within the boundary of the component without affecting other components. Every attempt is made to minimize any dependency on the development or deployment environments, especially the user interface. There should be no logic within the business component that is specific to any display of the information within the classes; that logic must lie in user interface components.

There are two other kinds of business component: *wrappers and adaptors*. A wrapper, as its name implies, wraps up the functionality of an existing system. An adaptor not only encapsulates existing functionality but also provides extra features.

Data component

A *data component* is a kind of component that acts as a bridge between mainly business components and the database services. It is recommended that for every business component there is a matching data component that handles the transformation of the persistent data within the classes of the business component to the appropriate database stored format, e.g. tables, rows, types.

This separation of responsibilities gives a number of benefits:

1 Business components are designed without the constraints of any database structure, making the business component more reusable in different data environments. This allows changes in either structures to be handled appropriately without major 'ripples' throughout the structures, e.g. changes in the database schema do not affect the business component structure.

2 Database information can be cached in its original format, e.g. Microsoft record set, within the data component to allow speedy updates to the stored structures. Caching also allows facilities to rollback or refresh information, e.g. changes in the business component's data may be reset, say by cancellation by the user, and can then be refreshed from the cached data.

3 Data handling can be more efficient when, for example, there is no data to be stored in the database. This is handled by the business component only notifying the data component when any persistent data (attribute) is changed, then when the business component wants to commit any data it simply notifies the data component to commit, and if there has been no change, the data component replies 'done' otherwise the business data are stored as normal.

4 Data components handle the data for <u>one</u> business component, so that when a number of business components are involved in a transaction, then the transaction controller (a technical component) manages the 'commit scope' by sequencing the appropriate data components.

There is a negative side to the use of data components, however. The extra number of components means increased development effort, more components to instantiate, i.e. a data component for every business component, and perhaps slower performance as the persistent data are moved between the business and data components. Despite these downsides, the separate data component principle is recommended.

Technical component

A constructed component providing a set of technical services that are used mainly by business or user components, e.g. an error handler, or a security manager. This is a type of component that provides 'glue' that binds the business components to the system infrastructure. Technical components can also provide common services that are used throughout the organization, e.g. security management (log-on, log-off.) These are some typical technical components:

- error handler
- security manager
- XML packer and unpacker
- session and application management
- fail overload balancing
- cross (architecture) layer communication.

Technical components are delivered as part of technical architecture delivery.

Service

A service is a function that can be invoked using defined protocols and mechanisms. The service is usually a publicly exposed part of a larger application that resides on a different computational device (node) situated anywhere in the world, and that service may be provided by a third party. Web services are a typical form of this type of service provision, where web-based protocols and mechanisms are used by software elements to communicate with the service. The service is generally published as a *service interface*, with *service methods* (like the business services and interface of a component.)

During design, a service or group of services is modeled as a *component* in order that the interactions with other components can be determined and its deployment can be mapped. For example, a set of services provided by a financial company such as Dun & Bradstreet that check an individual's creditworthiness would be modeled as a single component (D&B) with the various services added as interfaces. The component is treated as a black box: no other design within the component is needed unless modifications to the services are required. If modifications or enhancements are required, then a *wrapper* or *adaptor* component is designed and constructed.

Technical architecture delivery

Technical architecture delivery involves the delivery of technical components and frameworks that support the use and maintenance of information within the technical environment. It is expressed in the same terms as the design of a business solution, using UML diagrams and component models. However, the range of products delivered to support the technical architecture is wider than those from a business solution project. In addition, technical architecture includes the concepts of *base classes*, *facility classes*, and *patterns* in its definitions.

Technical architecture model

The technical architecture model is a collection of diagrams that provide the shape of the technical architecture or framework. It contains use cases, object sequence diagrams, class diagrams, data models, etc. that represent the design of the technical framework solution. This is used to communicate the design and construction of the framework between the different team members involved in the use or reuse of the architecture.

A *technical architecture* provides the organizational structure that supports the behavior of the business application. This support is provided in the form of *base* and *facility classes*, which are used by the solution and component developers in the construction of their components; *technical components*, which provide services to the business components, e.g. error handling, and security validation; and *interfacing mechanisms* to other systems.

The technical architecture model defines the analysis and design of these parts. It evolves through a series of stages or iterations:

1 *Use cases* define the functional specification.

2 *Class models* outline the various stereotypes required by the solution.

3 *OSDs* document the interactions between the stereotypes and the classes.

4 Class diagrams are refined to show the design of the base and facility classes.

5 *Component* (*class*) *diagrams* show collections of facility classes combined to provide services.

6 *OSDs* are used to validate the interaction between the parts.

These are not all developed at one time; it is usual to provide the base/facility classes and technical components on a 'just-in-time' basis for the design/build of the business use cases. This is part of *increment planning* for the technical architecture. Planning is based on the priority of the business use cases (as determined by the stakeholders.) It is usual to provide a simple 'spike' solution that delivers a thin-slice prototype. Technical classes and components are needed to support this slice.

Technical architecture stereotype catalog

This catalog lists the technical architecture stereotypes that may be used in the design of a solution. A stereotype is the *classification* of an element (in this case an object.) This classification implies the object's type and behavior (semantic impact) when the stereotype is assigned to other objects. For example, an interface controller stereotype would be assigned to an object that controlled the searching for customer data. Stereotypes act as a form of 'shorthand' when assembling solutions.

Examples of *technical architecture stereotypes* are:

● *Visual presentation manager*: manages the visual presentation of data and the capturing of user changes and requests.

● *Interface controller*: manages the interaction and sequence of visual presentations. One good example of this is a GUI wizard that opens, manages and closes a number of visual presentations to a set business sequence.

● *Process object or use case controller*: abstracts the business process sequence rules into a single object for the use case, managing the interactions with the business objects rather than placing this business sequence intelligence in the GUI.

● *Transaction controller*: manages the interactions with the data services when a transaction is used. Starts and ends the transaction, and notifies participating business and data objects when a transaction fails.

● *Database connector*: manages and controls the database connection(s) for an application.

Base and facility classes

These are a set of classes provided by the technical architecture team that are used in the construction of a component or solution. Base classes provide generic *functionality*, which can be inherited by objects of a particular type, e.g. business or visual control classes. Facility classes provide generic *facilities*, which are included and used by objects and components in a solution, e.g. object manager, component broker, interface controller.

Stereotypes are identified during the analysis of the technical architecture and are then transformed into base or facility classes during the design stage of the workflow. Base classes are used in the design of both the component contents and the solution, where each concrete class is a realization of a stereotype. Facility classes are concrete classes that provide common behavior (services) to the component or solution.

Technical architecture patterns

This is a set of patterns that provide generic solutions for common technical architecture requirements, e.g. error handling. A pattern is a generic description of *how* a problem can be solved. Designers take the patterns and apply them to the context in which they are working. The context may serve to alter the structure or content of the pattern to some extent. Patterns can be viewed as learning aids, as they document the typical way that a given problem is solved within the organization. Design patterns are described as:

> A design pattern systematically names, motivates, and explains a general design that addresses a recurring design problem in object-oriented systems. It describes the problem, the solution, when to apply the solution, and its consequences. It also gives implementation hints and examples. The solution is a general arrangement of objects and classes that solve the problem. The solution is customized and implemented to solve the problem in a particular context.
>
> [Gamma *et al.*]

Select Perspective Patterns comprises a comprehensive set of technical architecture patterns, models, stereotypes, and base and facility classes.

Manage

Managing components is the pivot in the supply–manage–consume model. Component or services supply activities are the responsibilities of component suppliers, whether they are internal or external to the organization. Certification, publication, and maintenance activities are the responsibility of the component management team. Finding, evaluating, and applying are the responsibilities of the component or service consumers.

Component and service management requires a clear reuse strategy and approach, and tools that automate the process such as publication, notification, and tracking of component or service reuse.

Reuse strategy

This defines the strategy for adopting reuse within the organization. Like anything strategic, this is something vital that is intended to last a long time. Within the reuse strategy, there are four key sections that need to be defined:

1 *What is meant by reuse*: this means identifying the things that you want to reuse, such as designs, components, services, frameworks, and architectures, and how you want to reuse them, e.g. black box or white box.

2 *Populating a library of reusable assets*: this covers the identification and prioritization of assets that are useful to the business, e.g. business services. It defines how these assets will be acquired and from what sources, whether internal or external, and the policies for certification, classification, and storage.

3 *Sharing reusable assets*: this covers the communication mechanisms regarding the contents of the library or repository, and how they will be located and retrieved. This may also involve defining the documentation, which is expected to assist in understanding and reusing the located asset.

4 *Maintaining reusable assets*: this defines the maintenance policy for assets and the notification procedures for assets reusers. It covers responsibility for correcting any defects, backwards compatibility, and versioning.

Without setting such a strategy, reuse may happen in an *ad hoc* and uncoordinated way that wastes the scarce resources of the organization through duplicated effort and multiple solutions for common problems.

Classification scheme

The classification scheme defines the chosen method and information stored with a component that aids its location and retrieval. Having large numbers of reusable components in a library is useless unless they can be found. This problem has been faced by others such as library sciences, botany, and zoology, and each has developed a scheme for classification. Unfortunately, there are few corresponding schemes for software components at the present time.

One approach is to classify according to the different domains, whether business, infrastructure, enterprise, etc. There will be overlaps, but each developer knows where to look. Another approach is to consider using a scheme based on keywords/attributes. The keywords are chosen by the component producer, with no restraint on the number and structure of words. There may also be a dictionary of the keyword vocabulary for selection. When attributes are used in the scheme, they are usually a small set of predefined values such as author, creation date, etc. Most reuse libraries use a combination of keywords and attributes.

A more formal scheme is based on *facets* of the component. Facets describe basic categories or dimensions of a particular domain. When the domain is for the component or service, then the four categories are:

1 *abstraction*: a noun, e.g. stack, flight manager;

2 *services*: description of the operations, e.g. arithmetic, manipulation, data entry;

3 *operates on*: what does it need to act with;

4 *dependencies*: non-functional dependencies that may make the component difficult to reuse.

Whichever scheme is chosen, it is important to monitor the effectiveness of the classification to ensure that assets may be found quickly and successfully.

Reusable software catalog

This is a published list of various software assets that may be reused when forming solutions. It includes the component library, but it can also include other descriptions of different reusable assets, such as SQL strings, designs, and databases schemata.

Locating these assets depends on the schemes for classification (see Classification Scheme), representation, storage, and communication. Most developers look to find possible assets from descriptions of their requirements, which may not be the same classification under which the asset has been stored. As a result, many location schemes in catalogs are based on searching for matching attributes using:

- wild card searches
- thesaurus of synonyms
- phrase searching
- Boolean combination of criteria
- automatic stemming, where a word is reduced to its root and all derivatives identified.

It is common for the catalog to be separate from the actual storage of the reusable software assets. This separation means that library-based tools with sophisticated matching algorithms can be used rather than typical storage mechanisms, e.g. file directories.

Certified component

This is a component that has been through the approved certification process within the component management activity. Certification ensures that reusable components meet some level of quality. This engenders trust in the component so that developers can be confident that an independent evaluation of the component has been done. But what happens if that process is slow, or components are needed promptly? Most successful certification schemes issue levels of certification with the reusable component:

- *Level 1*: no testing, no documentation, level of completeness unknown;
- *Level 2*: level of completeness verified;
- *Level 3*: test cases and test suites provided and executed;
- *Level 4*: fully tested, and documented, and meets all quality criteria.

Obviously, a developer would be wary of a Level 1 certified component, but if the reusable component is potentially useful then the developer may take the risk. This risk is clearly identified from the level of certification.

Component metrics set

This set of metrics records the various targets used to evaluate the return on investment (ROI) on component or service reuse. The essential component metrics set comprises:

- *creation costs*: cost in creating or preparing a component for reuse;
- *threshold*: number of times that component must be reused to recover costs;
- *usage costs*: measures the reuser-related costs incurred each time a component is reused; includes finding, understanding, modifying, and integrating,
- *target level*: minimum proportion of a system that is reusable;
- *maintenance costs*: costs of supporting the component; for producers and for reusers;
- *commonality*: how frequently the component occurs across a set or family of systems;
- *actual reuse*: record of number of times the component has been reused on a project;
- *popularity*: number of times the component has been examined (retrieved) for possible reuse.

Without such a set of metrics to collect and evaluate, the effectiveness of component or service reuse is difficult to quantify.

Consume

Consume is an umbrella process for all the main workflows that deliver business solutions as part of a project. This means that it covers business alignment, business architecture, technical architecture integration, solution delivery, and solution rollout.

Business alignment

Business alignment ensures that the intended IT solution meets the needs of the business by providing a formalized view of the requirements for a solution; this is known as the *domain model*. Communication remains the key to this more formal view, so it is still expressed in concepts that are meaningful to the end-user, e.g. business process models. Based on this view, the boundary of the IT solution is identified and the system requirements are defined.

Domain model

The domain model refers to a collection of models, catalogs, documents, etc. that are created and used during business alignment. This collection aims to provide sufficient detail for the component and solution development activities.

One or more of these items are part of the collection:

- vision statement
- as-is business process model
- to-be business process model
- business rules catalog
- domain catalog (a list of supporting material, such as document examples)
- use case model
- non-functional requirements.

Business process model

This model contains a collection of business process thread and process hierarchy diagrams that show the flow of activities for a business process. The model may reflect the 'as-is 'activities within the business and/or may define the 'to-be' design for planned process improvements.

The *business process model* consists of a set of business processes, scoped according to the needs of the development project of the organization as a whole. For example, if a sales support application is being developed, it may be decided that only the business processes relating to sales need to be modeled. The standard definition of a business process is: 'a collection of activities that takes one or more inputs and creates an output that is of value to the customer'.

Individual business processes are modeled using a graphical notation to represent activities (grouped into processes), the events that trigger them and their resulting output. Two types of diagram are used to model business processes. The first is the process hierarchy diagram, which is used to show how activities are made up of smaller activities. Second, the process thread diagram can be used to show, for any given group of activities:

- the event that triggers the activities;
- the order in that the activities take place, shown as transitions; and
- the result of the activities.

Diagrams for the business process model should be supported by textual descriptions of all diagram elements. For example, each event, activity, and result needs to be described using the language of the business.

Using these diagrams, it is possible to define the scope of the planned system solution, and to map the activities or tasks (known as elementary business processes) to use cases (see use case model) that define the functional requirements of the new solution. This traceability ensures that the planned solution remains aligned with the business needs.

In process modeling exercises that take place as part of a business change program, for example during the implementation of a new computer system or application, it may be necessary to produce two sets of models, namely:

1 as-is business models showing the current business processes;

2 to-be business models showing the planned business processes.

The to-be business process models may well be the outputs of a business process improvement (BPI) exercise. Depending on how such an exercise is conducted, the process models may well evolve throughout the lifetime of the exercise.

Use case model

This model describes the functional requirements of a system in terms of use cases. It consists of a series of UML diagrams, each of which represents a set of usage scenarios ('use cases') involving the users of the system (the 'actors') and their interactions with the system. Each use case contains a description in the form of a series of interactions between the actor and the system.

There is at least one use case diagram (UCD) for every system or application showing the actors who are to use the system, and the functionality that they expect. Most projects have a number of use case diagrams that capture different aspects of the system. For example, on a project with many types of user there may be a UCD for each actor.

However, diagrams are not enough; each use case should also have a full set of details. The central purpose of the use case is to describe the series of interactions between the actor and the application; these are described textually in pairs of:

● the actor's request of the application

● the application's response to the request.

Additional information can also be created for the use case, such as its intent, preconditions and post-conditions; see guidelines reference below.

The use case model can be developed iteratively, as a series of increments. Early increments are likely to be more abstract, describing the actor and the application in conceptual terms. As understanding of the application requirements and the solution progresses and improves, use cases will become more concrete, for example describing the mechanisms to be used to enable the interaction to take place.

Use cases are key to:

● the organization of work structured in the project;

● the planning, management and control of the project;

● the construction, testing, and delivery of the software;

● the management of changes in requirements.

Large use case models with many use cases and actors can quickly come to resemble a spider's web of crossing lines. Partitioning the model across several diagrams can mitigate this effect. The most effective way to partition the model is on a by-actor basis; each diagram contains a single actor and the use cases they are permitted to invoke.

Quality metric definitions

These are a set of standards that define the attributes associated with quality (how well) and how they are measured.

Many requirements are defined in an imprecise way, e.g. 'the system must be easy to use'. Easier to whom? A novice, a occasional user, an expert? Unless and until such a statement is specified more accurately, then the gap in expectations may cause the resulting solution to be rejected by the users. To be precise in specifying requirements, it is important to separate *function* (what has to be built) from *quality* (how well it must be built.) For example, a 'readable user manual' is actually two requirements: a user manual (a function delivered or not) and readable (a quality attribute).

Quality metric definitions define a hierarchy of attribute categories, e.g. usability, and the quantifiable values for that attribute, e.g. time to proficiency = 2 days. These quality metrics provide the list of key attributes and their specifications. This is a dynamic picture, as these can change over time as the solution evolves and delivers increasing functionality. These attributes are characteristics of our planned solution that represent constraints, to reach a certain minimum level without spending too many resources in attaining that level.

Each quality attribute has the following format:[1]

- *scale*: the scale of the measure specification, e.g. number of user errors;
- *test*: a practical test or measuring tool used to determine a value for the scale;
- *worst*: worst acceptable limit on the scale; i.e. a failure;
- *plan*: the expected level on the scale;
- *now*: some currently existing value for comparison with delivered solution (optional);
- *source*: link to reference material or expert.

Careful consideration of the attributes and their values, perhaps after negotiation, ensures that the designers and developers provide appropriate solutions that meet the quality standards. For example, if the usability metric states 'less than two hours to become proficient with the new system', then the user interface may be designed to reflect the current layout of the paper documents, and that the existing user interface technology, such as Microsoft Windows, is used.

Non-functional requirements

Non-functional requirements define all of the forces on the application in development that do not relate to its functionality. These include quality requirements, external constraints, and business rules.

1. A detailed example is shown in the full version of Select Perspective.

The non-functional requirements on an application are as important as the functional requirement, as they dictate the criteria by which the functional requirements will be judged. For example, a functional requirement may be that customers should be able to enter their own details. However, it is the non-functional requirements that will specify the turnaround time for logging the details, the platform upon which the functionality depends and the number of customers that can log their details in parallel.

The following can all be considered as types of non-functional requirement:

- *Business rules*, or the *constraints* imposed by the business on the application – for example, the fact that customers qualify for special treatment after they have spent a certain amount of money with the company.

- *External constraints* – for example the fact that the company has standardized on a certain hardware or software platform, for example, 'the database is to be Oracle.'

- *Quality requirements*, such as usability, performance, availability, reliability security, and maintainability; these are described below.

It is possible to define the above for both the application as a whole – for example, 'the availability of the application needs to equate to one hour downtime per year' – and against individual functions of the application – 'to comply with national law, all new customers need to be credit checked before their details are entered'.

Non-functional requirements will vary from application to application. In general, all quality requirements will hold for all applications (for example, all applications need to be usable.) However, their level of applicability will change; for example, some systems need to be more available than others. There are many possible quality requirements; here are the more common ones:

- *Usability*: use of the application should be intuitive, and the amount of training required to use the system should be minimized.

- *Performance*: the application should be able to respond within a given time frame to a request from a user or another system.

- *Availability*: the amount of time that an application is in an unusable state (for example, due to failure or maintenance) should be kept to a minimum.

- *Reliability*: the likelihood of an application failure, through software bugs or hardware failure, should be minimized.

- *Security*: the application should have sufficient protection against information privacy or loss through external tampering.

- *Maintainability*: the application should be designed in such a way that upgrades and other changes can be made with minimum disruption.

Other potential quality requirements are *connectivity, configurability, and adaptability*. It is up to individual projects to select the most appropriate categories for quality requirements.

Descriptions of quality requirements are often vague and imprecise. A common example is 'must be fast'. For a programmer fast is measured in milliseconds, but for a user fast may mean 'faster than now', and five seconds is acceptable. The solution is to describe non-functional requirements as a 'how well' list. Examples of these are given in *quality metric definitions*.

Non-functional requirements are as important as the functional requirements, where the effort tends to be focused. Unless and until the non-functional requirements have been considered and documented in detail, the full requirements cannot be known.

Test strategy

The test strategy is a risk-driven strategy that ensures that scarce test resources are deployed effectively and efficiently. It sets out the overall approach for ensuring that the solution, or elements of it, are validated to the satisfaction of its stakeholders. It takes into account the law of diminishing returns, and therefore it should be based on ensuring that the risks in the *risk register* are mitigated. It is based on the philosophy that testing should be directed at showing the presence rather than the absence of errors.

Resources available for testing are always limited. The role of the test strategy is to ensure that resources are targeted at solution areas most likely to yield testing value, and hence a demonstrable level of quality assurance. For example, there is no point in using all available resources to build a comprehensive scalability-testing framework if it leaves no resource for testing the application functionality.

The test strategy sets out the plan for ensuring that the solution, or elements of it, are validated to the satisfaction of its stakeholders. Each stakeholder group will require a different perspective on testing, for example:

- *Unit tests*, to verify the quality of components as they are produced to satisfy component managers.
- *Increment tests*, to verify the quality of a given internal delivery of an increment, for example compilation tests, integration tests.
- *Solution tests*, to verify the quality of whole solution deliveries prior to their deployment, to the satisfaction of the deployment manager.
- *User acceptance tests*, to verify that the functional requirements have been met and that the system is usable, to the satisfaction of user representatives. In general, these map onto use cases.
- *Operational tests* to verify the non-functional and management requirements of the solution to satisfy system management staff. For example, installation and upgrade features can be tested.

Each of these facets of the test strategy requires an ensemble of test cases – a test suite – and the necessary supporting mechanisms to run them, as follows:

- *Levels of testing to be performed*: for each test-related process, a definition of the techniques, resources, outputs and tools required.
- *Test coverage targets*: the extent to which system structure, behavior and environment are to be tested:
  - For system structure, coverage measures should be defined for all identified system interfaces.
  - For system behavior, coverage measures should include functional and non-functional aspects of system behavior.
  - For system environment, coverage measures should include live, 'pseudo-live' and user environments, operation in normal and extreme business use, rare events and use of live data.
- *Test management and procedures*: relating to test specification, execution, test recording and management, error reporting and tracking, etc.
- *Test environment definitions*: covering the equipment requirements and setup procedures for the test environment.

Note that testing does not have to be a one-shot operation. In the iterative, incremental processes that are usually employed for CBD, testing is integrated throughout the development life cycle. The test strategy should take into account the law of diminishing returns, i.e. the premise that it is impossible to test any system or application fully.

The scale and expected results of testing may vary depending on the stage of the project that has been reached. For example, early alpha tests can be performed by the (often internal) stakeholder who ordered the system; later beta tests are pre-release tests, usually conducted by general users or selected customers.

Business architecture

Using any business process models and the requirements model it is possible to abstract a view of the overall business architecture. Three distinct architectural views – process, responsibility, and information – can be analyzed in the existing models and integrated to form a set of candidate *business components* and the dependencies between them. Business components are the crucial element of the architecture. Once these components have been identified in terms of their name, purpose, and main responsibilities, the first attempt at finding a suitable component or service can be made. Suitable components or services may be reused from the component repository, which in turn may introduce constraints that require further refinement of the business architecture.

The main objective of the business architecture is to provide a stable basis from which to begin the major development activities.

Business architecture model

This model is a collection of UML diagrams that specify the analysis and design of the *business components* for a solution. It contains use cases, object sequence diagrams, class diagrams, and data models that represent the components and their relationships in the business layer of the solution. It may also include collaboration and state diagrams if these are useful.

The *business architecture model* describes the overall solution, the services required and ensures that the business components support 80–90 percent of the functional requirements (the basic course and most important alternative courses.)

This model will, if designed correctly, define a long-term business architecture that enables the project manager and development team to build incrementally without compromising the system as a whole. Once this activity has been completed, parallel development can be undertaken as functionality is clearly cohesive with all the interfaces defined.

- A series of business components have been found:
  — each component has limited dependencies with other components;
  — each component is described.
- Interaction diagrams are present for each use case:
  — the basic course is modeled;
  — the alternative courses for each use case have at least been thought through.
- Each service has been defined:
  — descriptions, post-conditions, preconditions, and constraints are defined;
  — parameters and exceptions are described.

The business architecture model defines the requirements for all the business components and services.

Technical architecture integration

Technical architecture is a key requirement for the successful delivery of contemporary solutions. It ensures that a common technical environment is defined, communicated, reused, enhanced, and maintained across multiple projects.

Should an existing and suitable architecture not exist, then the technical architecture is assembled and delivered as part of the supply process; this is known as technical architecture delivery. *Technical architecture integration* is the application of the technical architecture to multiple development projects. As each project is executed, the technical architecture is assessed in terms of its fitness for purpose, gaps that must be filled, and additional technical issues introduced by the project.

Technical architecture requirement

The technical architecture requirement defines the tools, environments and software solutions to be used for the project. Technical architecture needs to take into account the use of objects, components, middleware, legacy systems, and common off-the-shelf (COTS) software. This includes the use of web server and application servers and their collection into web farms: the *deployment architecture*.

Also defined are the principles of its design. Is it to be highly flexible, maintainable, high-performance, highly reliable, highly robust or what percentages of all of these? This is based on the architecture's responsibilities and participation in the non-functional requirements for the solution (and organization.) Some example requirements follow.

- *Flexibility*: the application must be configurable for different customers. This may apply in one or more of the following areas:
  — enabling of relevant functions only;
  — support for different configuration of the user interface for different customers, through menus, toolbars and grids;
  — support for, and customer control of, different languages for the user interface;
  — extensibility of business properties for a customer;
  — configurability of user interface parameters (e.g. colors, form positions) and storage of these between user sessions.
- *Portability*: there is limited need for portability of applications at this stage. However, in future it may be necessary to use a different database for persistent storage or place the application, or parts of it, on different hardware and operating system platforms.
- *Performance*: simple tasks (i.e. those operating on a single object) should execute as fast as possible – within three seconds in all cases. Other more complex tasks must normally be completed within thirty seconds. The application must perform to this standard even when communication over a wide area network is necessary. Meeting this requirement is subject to the WAN latency.
- *Scalability*: the application must be designed to work well with one or two users working locally or with up to 100 users working in a client–server environment.
- *Concurrency*: multiple user access must leave data in a consistent state. It must be possible to reflect data changes made by one user on the views being accessed by another user, without user intervention.
- *Maintainability*: a key requirement is to build easily maintained application code. Reducing the time and cost of repairs and making enhancements is a key aim. To improve maintainability, all interfaces must be properly designed, documented and tested. Wherever possible, tools and templates are required to simplify and standardize the construction of new code. Design and supporting documentation should promote component reuse. Components should be published to allow both the component specification and the implementations to be cataloged in a flexible manner that facilitates easy search and retrieval.

Technical architecture specification

This specifies the technical architecture using *technical use cases* to define the functions required and provide traceability from the project requirements to the constructed technical components. The specification can also define the non-functional requirements to be supported. Some examples of non-functional requirements (categorized into performance, flexibility, maintainability, reliability and robustness) are shown in Table 10.1

Solution delivery

One of the key deliverables in solution delivery workflow is the *solution architecture*, which provides a comprehensive overview of the structure of the proposed solution. It is an analysis model that may be seen as the blueprint for the solution. Following completion of the solution architecture, the solution itself can then be implemented as a series of incremental deliveries of the solution, each of which will have its own *solution model*. As such, the solution architecture model covers the breadth of requirements, functional and non-functional, collated for the solution.

Test cases are another important deliverable, as they ensure confidence in the delivered solution. It may also be necessary to construct a *thin-slice prototype* to make informed decisions about the technology, the process, and the teams.

Table 10.1   Some examples of non-functional requirements

Non-functional requirement	Category (P/F/M/R/Ro)	Notes
Browser client without local functionality	P/F/Ro	The use of a browser without local functionality eliminates any applets or cookies to speed the configuration of the navigation or management of business process. This impacts performance, as continuous reloads of subsequent views is required, but it increases flexibility as any browser (including casual internet cafes, mobile phones, and Digital TV connections) can use the booking service.
Multiple Web Server Farm	P/R/Ro	As the components may be instantiated on different servers between client requests, use of the application object and session object needs to be examined, as these will not traverse servers, only stay resident on each server.

Solution architecture specification

The solution architecture specification defines the structure of the proposed solution and specifies how it will be built. It provides a logical and physical view of the solution, and presents technology options to support it.

Solution architecture specifications describe the solution from an architectural standpoint. It is defined to meet the functional requirements of the application specified in the use case model, together with the non-functional requirements such as business rules, qualities, and constraints. The specification consists of:

- a description of the solution
- a logical view of the solution
- a physical view of the solution
- technology options for the solution.

These are described in detail in the following sections.

Solution description

This is a general description of the solution in terms of:

- The type of application to be implemented, for example whether the application is customer-facing or supplier-facing, who will be the users of the application, and how they will access it.
- General constraints on the application, for example which existing infrastructure elements it needs to take into account.
- The approach to solution deployment, for example whether it will be delivered in phases.
- A general indication of how the quality requirements of the solution will be met, introducing logical and physical aspects of the solution.

The solution architecture specification should be developed iteratively. Clearly, it is necessary to fix the solution architecture prior to developing it. However, in the early stages of the project there may be several technology options, each of which imposes different logical and physical constraints on the solution. The different elements of the solution architecture are mutually impacting, for example the selected logical architecture will impact on the choice of technologies, and *vice versa*.

Logical view of the solution

This describes the architecture of the solution from a logical perspective. For example, the architecture could be client–server, three tier or distributed. The specification should describe the selected architecture, then it should show how it will be applied to the specific solution. For example, a diagram could be drawn showing the logical elements of the architecture, and how they interface with the users of the application and the external systems to be linked.

Physical view of the solution

This describes the architecture in terms of how the logical elements of the solution map onto the physical software and hardware elements of the solution. Descriptions of the technology types need to be provided; for example, the physical view should talk in terms of application servers, databases, firewalls and communications links. The physical view is best represented as a hardware diagram showing how the physical elements relate to each other, together with explanatory scenarios showing how the architecture works in practice.

Technology options

Technologies need to be selected to support the solution itself. There will be a number of choices for each of the physical elements of the solution, some of which may be selected in isolation but some of which will be interdependent. For example, it may be decided to select a single-vendor software solution (for example, Microsoft); however, there will always be elements that the vendor does not provide and hence care must be taken to ensure that all dependencies are understood and addressed.

Also, technologies are required to support the development of the solution; these include development environments, testing tools and configuration management tools.

Solution architecture model

The solution architecture model describes the architectural shape of the solution. It provides an external view of the complete solution architecture, but it does not descend into the internal design of the solution. Key diagrams are use cases, object sequence diagrams, and class and component diagrams.

Solution architecture models provide a comprehensive overview of the architecture of the proposed solution. It is an analysis model that may be seen as the blueprint for the solution. Following completion of the solution architecture, the solution itself can then be implemented as a series of incremental deliveries of the solution, each of which will have its own solution model. As such, the solution architecture model should cover the breadth of requirements collated for the solution, both functional and non-functional.

The solution architecture model evolves through a series of iterations, in which the depth of the model is increased. It consists of the following diagrams:

- Use cases define the functional requirements to be met by the solution.
- Component (class) diagrams outline the various components required by the solution in terms of services they provide and the classes they contain.
- Object sequence diagrams (OSDs) document the relationship between the use cases and the components.

Early iterations of the model will relate the main flow through the use cases to business services from the components. Later iterations will cover alternative flows and will show interactions between both business and technical components. The solution architecture model shows the classes contained by the components, but it does not show the internals of the components.

Solution model

The solution model consists of a set of UML diagrams that describe the design of the solution from a number of perspectives. These include a static view of the solution (i.e. its composition), a dynamic view (i.e. its behavior) and views corresponding to how information is stored and the solution is deployed. Key diagrams are class diagrams, object sequence diagrams (OSDs), state diagrams, deployment diagrams and a persistent data model.

This model clearly defines the software solution devised to meet a cohesive set of functional and non-functional requirements. The solution model can refer to the whole solution to meet the complete set of use cases, or a single increment corresponding to a subset of use cases. In either case, the solution model defines the scope of what is to be delivered. The solution model consists of the following diagrams:

- class diagrams showing user classes, component interfaces, utility classes, external interfaces, and the relationships between them;
- object sequence diagrams (OSDs), which show the thread of control through the solution (for particular use cases);
- persistent data model, which defines the stored entities;
- state diagrams for complex situations, e.g. error recovery;
- deployment diagrams showing the location of the system parts.

In addition, the solution model can include:

- additional architectural information, for example the external infrastructure elements upon which the solution depends;
- user interface prototypes showing how the user interface is likely to be constructed;
- supporting information, such as constraints and dependencies.

It is important that all elements of a solution model be consistent. Delivery of the solution model needs to ensure consistency between the diagrams involved, as well as with external elements such as those mentioned above. Planning of the solution architecture is based on the priority of the business use cases (as determined by the stakeholders.) It is usual to provide a simple 'spike' solution that delivers a thin-slice prototype. For example, in the Select Cruise system the first increment would be Make an Inquiry, the second Make Booking, and the final increment Send Mailings.

Test case

A test case is a repeatable series of tests used to determine whether one particular part of the system works properly. These parts or elements may vary in size and complexity, ranging from a component or service to a complete solution. The exact nature of the test case will vary according to the type of element that is to be tested.

A test case may contain several testing activities or steps, which are conducted in sequence to verify the particular element of the system. The test case may be seen as similar to a use case in that it is a behaviorally related sequence of interactions, but it does not restrict itself to user interactions with the system. Test cases can exist for internal system elements as well as for the whole system.

There are several types of test case, such as component tests, operational tests, solution tests, and user acceptance tests. These are described in the *test strategy*. The following needs to be defined for each test case:

- *test case steps*: the activities involved in the test case;
- *input data*: information to be used as input to the test case;
- *expected results*: information or behavior expected as output from the test case.
- *test environment*: the context in which the test needs to be carried out, for example hardware and software requirements;
- *constraints*: for example, the presence of specific facilities;
- *additional scenarios*: there may be several ways in which a test case can be executed.

Test cases can be combined into a *test suite*, which runs all tests of a specified type. This is defined in the test specification for that type of testing; for example, the *solution test specification* defines the solution test suite. The test specification should indicate when the test suite needs to be run, for example following a major change, at a significant point in the development cycle or prior to a major release.

Thin-slice prototype

This is the smallest possible 'core' solution built in the shortest possible time. It is used to inform decisions about technology, the domain, design, process, and team capabilities. The rationale for thin slices[2] is that when working in a new problem domain or with a new technology you do not understand, and you cannot create an initial design in which you can place much confidence, then developing a thin-slice prototype will give you the understanding and confidence in your understanding and team capabilities.

This prototype can work at any level: objects, components, subsystems, and solutions. If you are fortunate, the prototype will naturally extend into your final system. However, you will still have to adapt the solution for the myriad of actual variations that make the domain complex.

Solution rollout

During incremental development, only a few of the solution releases will be rolled onto the operational platform for use by the business users. While

2. Also known as 'spikes' by the eXtreme Programming community.

successful rollout depends on operational procedures, migration strategy, and test plans, the critical delivery for component- and service-based development is the deployment model. This model documents the placement of the software components on the various parts of the operational environment.

Deployment model

This is a collection of diagrams that show the planned and/or actual deployment of software artifacts and components within the operational environment. The *deployment model* represents the planned and actual location and relationships between the runtime parts of the solution, i.e. the components. In UML, this is presented as a *deployment diagram*, which is a static structure of the nodes and their connections. From the UML specification, a deployment diagram is defined as:

> a graph of nodes connected by communication associations. A node represents a run-time computational resource, which generally has at least a memory and often computational capability. Nodes may contain component instances. This indicates that the component lives or runs on the node and as the component may contain objects it also indicates that the objects reside on that node.
>
> [OMG-UML, V1.x]

This deployment diagram is normally created when planning the deployment; it does not show the *actual* relationships unless the deployer physically maintains and updates the diagram.

In Select Component Manager, it is possible to show the planned and the actual deployment. This is presented as a *deployment tree* diagram showing the nodes and under each node the list of deployed components and a list of associated nodes, i.e. the dependencies. This deployment tree diagram can be created by dragging and dropping components into nodes. After the physical deployment has taken place and any adjustments/changes have been made to the operational environment, e.g. new components added, updates to the runtime support such as IBM Websphere, then these can be synchronized with the original deployment tree to show the actual deployment. It is obviously possible to synchronize with an empty tree to get the existing deployed components into Select Component Manager.

Solution release

This is a validated and verified build of a solution that can be deployed. Deployment may be to new or existing users, or to production/live facilities, or to training locations.

A *release* is a version of a piece of software that has been made public as opposed to a version that is in development, or otherwise unreleased. A release is a major release, a revision, or a 'bug-fix', and it may then be deployed into one or more locations.

Summary

Select Perspective is a delivery-based approach to contemporary software development. This means that only those deliverables of value to the project need to be produced, and scarce resources are allocated effectively. This chapter covered key deliverables in component- and service-based development.

Tools 11

Numerous tools are used during a CBD project, many of which are common to all types of software development project. This chapter focuses on those tools that are specifically used in a component- or service-based development approach. Often, software vendors bundle tools that provide 'point solutions' into offerings with a much wider applicability. In line with the topic of this book and Select Perspective, component- and service-based bundles are of specific interest. General application development suites will therefore not be considered, in favor of component- and service-oriented tools. Component factories will be outlined first, with more detail on the constituent parts in the following sections.

Component factories

Component factories are typically suites of tools that encompass requirements management, visual modeling, component management, quality assurance, application assembly and deployment. They differ from general modeling tools and integrated development environments (IDEs) in their level of abstraction. Rather than focusing purely on objects and classes, component factories must also consider applications architectures, based on component, interfaces and services. This abstraction maps to contemporary concepts, such as the OMGs MDA, which distinguishes between three separate views: first, the 'computation-independent business model', which documents the business and its workflows; second, the 'platform-independent component view', which defines how components and services plug together to deliver an application; and, finally, the 'platform-specific component view', which details the component internals, such as classes and objects. All of these views are supported by Select Perspective, as you will have seen in the preceding chapters. Many tools on the market today provide good support for either business-level models or platform-specific views. However, tools vendors have capitalized on misinformation surrounding the OMG's MDA and suggested that their tools support the MDA mappings purely with template-driven code generation. However, only a few fill in the missing link, which focuses on solutions that are architected from components or services. At the time of going to print, the tools vendors delivering solutions in this space who should be considered include Aonix, Web Gain, Computer Associates and Wilde Technologies, to name just a few. Aonix's Select Business Solutions Division provides the most mature and proven component factory and is therefore worthy of consideration. It also provides complete support for Select Perspective, which has been introduced throughout this book.

Component managers

When applying Select Perspective or another software development process based upon components and services, a component manager role makes a great deal of sense. The productivity of a component manager is significantly enhanced when automated tooling is applied. Component management tools help to manage, publish and use components, speeding delivery of applications. The number of component management tools on the market is growing and is generally split along two axes: first, commercial versus commerce-free and, second, components stored on or off site. The commercial decision can easily be resolved by understanding your organization's structure. If component and service use is expected to occur across the divisional structure or between cost centers then you may need a component manager with commerce built in. However, this is not the norm, and most component management solutions are typically commerce-free, with security and access controls providing similar functionality. The location of hosting is a much more significant issue. Off-site hosting makes sense where the in-house IT resources are limited and the value of the components and services is relatively low. When the asset value is higher and you have the necessary hardware and staff, an on-site solution is always favorable.

Component management tools and UDDI servers are conceptually and functionally different, but we should expect them to merge over time. Current UDDI server limitations are based upon the highly abstract service definitions and the lack of real support for direct component architectures such as EJB and COM. True component management tools are therefore recommended and can be used on the same projects as UDDI servers but with a design-time focus.

Occasionally, confusion surrounds the difference between a source code control system and a component manager. At a conceptual level, source code control systems are highly granular (for example, a beach full of grains of sand.) Component managers contrast this by storing larger 'prefabricated' chunks of code; these have identifiable specifications for use and reuse. The reach of components and services within an organization may necessitate more process-oriented facilities than can be provided by a pure repository, e.g. registry of interest, specification searching, librarian control. Hopefully, your CBD endeavors will be highly successful, and scalability should therefore also be considered.

There are a growing number of component management tools on the market today, from vendors such as Aonix's Select Business Solutions, ComponentSource, Flashline, Computer Associates and Adaptive. Although they may appear to be identical at first glance, once you dig a little deeper you will find that they all do very different things. For example, this is highlighted by the partnership and integration between Aonix Select Component Manager and ComponentSource. Each of the two products fulfills a different role in the software development life cycle. Select Component Manager is the most advanced and mature of the component management tools at the time of going to print. In this tooling area, a detailed evaluation is recommended, and an excellent set of criteria can be found in the 'Component library' section of *Component Based Software Engineering* by Heineman and Council (2001).

Visual modeling tools

The standardization of modeling notations through OMG's Unified Modeling Language (UML) has had two primary effects for component- and service-based developers. First, the availability of object-oriented UML tools has exploded. At least 85 vendors now provide some form of UML modeling tool. Second, the object-oriented focus of UML has hindered the move to component- and service-based design. There are plans afoot, as there have been for quite some time, to introduce top-down component and service design concepts, via UML 2.0. Sadly, UML 1.x provides limited support for these concepts, although it has been the ratified standard since the late 1990s. OMG's MDA is a good response to this need but has yet to see true implementation by more than a handful of the visual modeling vendors. In making a recommendation for a visual modeling tool to support component- and service-based design, most of the currently well-known market brands should be ignored. They provide varying levels of UML 1.x support and inherently focus on low-level design requirements.

Therefore, tools from Rational, Popkin, Togethersoft and the like should probably be discounted. To achieve well-architected applications that utilize components and services, you need to consider vendors such as Aonix's Select Business Solutions, Wilde Technologies and Computer Associates. The primary requirements of a modeling tool for component- and service-based design are 'platform-independent component view' (Select Perspective Business Architecture) and tight integration with your component management repository for design-time reuse and component/service outsourcing. The key is to be able to communicate and agree your designs for application development before commencing construction. This reduces the overall cost of the project by finding problems earlier. Keeping designs up to date then provides benefits when you come to reuse or integrate component and services.

Select Component Architect (previously Select Enterprise) from Aonix's Select Business Solutions is an advanced tool set for modeling, designing and building next-generation enterprise applications. It has all the features and functionality you need to deliver high-quality component- and service-oriented applications quickly. Select Component Architect matches the Select Perspective exactly, so the concepts described in this book can easily be put into practice.

Requirements management

Requirements management tools allow all project stakeholders – including business analysts, product marketing, developers, testers and end-users – to collaborate on project requirements. Requirement input, versioning, actioning, and tracking are all important features of this type of tool. Good examples include Select Component Factory, Starbase's Caliber RM and Telelogic's DOORS.

This said, requirements management tools should only be used once the business demands are clearly understood. Don't forget that requirements management tools document the requirements for software systems, and even though you may feel that you are starting at the top, business workflows should be the real driver for software systems. Again, this concept has been highlighted earlier in the book, but it emphasizes the need to use a requirements management tool that links requirements not only to your system design and code but also to your desired business process designs.

Again, typical requirements management systems are not well suited to component- and service-based development. They can be applied to the overall requirements for the business IT system but need to be handled carefully for component specification. Component specifications have been defined earlier in this book and include diagrams as well as textural requirements.

Application assemblers

Application assembly relates to the physical implementation of the MDA 'platform-independent component view', or the Select Perspective 'business architecture'. This should be a relatively non-technical task that can be automated with tools such as Web Gain's Application Composer and Wilde Technologies. The intention for tools in this domain is to empower business specialists to compose applications from components built by software specialists. This is probably the most immature area of tooling within the CBD arena, but we expect to see a lot more tools available over the coming years.

The lower-level component assembly can also be considered for automation. Many modeling tools vendors provide framework code generation to accelerate the programming and increase the quality. One set of examples is the Aonix Select Business Solutions Language Pack extensions for Select Component Architect. These automate the generation of framework C#, VML Schema, Java, C++, and Visual Basic code, to name but a few. Existing or modified code can also be reverse engineered back into your Select Component Architect UML model. Unlike other round-trip engineering solutions, Language Packs (or Synchronizers) graphically differentiate between the model and the code, allowing selective synchronization.

Test managers

To ensure that the original component, service and application designs have been implemented correctly, test managers can be used to streamline the testing process. They can take their input from requirements and/or models to test finished code and applications. The additional considerations for automated testing, within a CBD project, focus on component sandboxing and service-level agreements (SLAs). This said, there are relatively few tools that focus specifically on CBD, and most popular test management tools are therefore satisfactory for this purpose.

The preceding sections have described the minimum components of a good component factory, but there are additional tools that may also be considered to accelerate your application construction and delivery. They are not mandatory and generally focus on improving the software development process, as can be seen by the following section on application animation.

Application animators

As the composition of business applications from services is key to the process of component- and service-based development, a new technique of application animation may also be useful. Alternative approaches to application animation include design-time visualization and rapid prototyping. These approaches are closer than they may first appear, as the primary difference is that prototyping takes more initial effort but provides richer animation examples. UML object sequence diagrams (OSD), with the OMT (Rumbaugh *et al.*) 'multi-scenario' extensions are a very powerful technique for designing and defining interacting components. However, they are not easy to communicate to end-users or customers. In Select Component Factory from Aonix Select Business Solutions, the Object Animator graphically walks through OSD scenarios. This helps to achieve user buy-in, as well as finding problems earlier in the software development life cycle, saving time and money later on.

Patterns

Patterns are gaining in popularity, thanks in part to Gamma *et al*. Although over-complicated through complex technical definitions, the concept of patterns is relatively useful in component- and service-based development. Select

Perspective provides a set of component patterns describing technical architecture components and their usage. The Select Perspective patterns were introduced briefly in Chapter 3 and are supplied as UML models within Select Component Factory.

O–R mapping

One of the most useful and longest standing patterns is that of object–relational (O–R) mapping (Rumbaugh *et al.*; Allen and Frost.) In a component- and service-oriented world, this could be renamed component–relational (C–R) mapping, but the concept is still very useful. As service-based architectures are conceptually different to pure data architectures, a defined mapping is necessary. The preceding chapter on Select Perspective's data architecture discussed 'data components', which wrap relational data with a service-/component-based architecture. Various tools are available for O–R mapping from vendors such as Aonix Select Business Solutions, Computer Associates and Rational. The 'Storage Mapper' in Select Component Factory is a good example; it automates the creation of relational database designs from the persistent objects in a UML class model. The impedance mismatch between OO and relational design (e.g. inheritance, primary keys) is resolved during generation. Once the relational database design has been created within the modeling tool, it can be generated as a relational database schema, via SQL DDL for example.

Project management tools

Project planning tools allow you to plan and track software development projects. The key to these types of tool is the communication of plans and collection of actual delivery dates. The best example available today is Microsoft Project. However, project management tools are also fairly generic and apply equally well to all types of software development project. One critical addition for service- and component-based development is that of outsourcing management. As component specifications can be delivered by developers who reside outside the consuming organization, overall project management is not advisable or practical. Each organization or sub-organization should manage only its own projects, but it must comply with an overall SMaC process, or project. This means that the component manager also plays a role in project management as component specifications are outsourced and finished components delivered. The implementation of Select Perspective SMaC implies sub-component project management and estimation, but it also has the opportunity to provide significant benefits through massively parallel development. In summary, for component- and service-based development, project management tools should be used in conjunction with a scalable (repository-based) component manager.

Process management and rollout tools

As you have seen from the preceding sections of this book, the main difference in component- and service-based development, when compared with OO, relational and structured development, is a conceptual process difference. Many of the techniques are similar, with slight variations in emphasis. This means that the biggest challenge is deploying mind-share among the software developers who are to apply these new concepts. A good place to start is to get all of the developers to read this book, but you will also need more depth and greater definition. Process management and rollout tools help by providing what is basically an electronic book that can be viewed by many developers from a single source. Consistency of approach can be achieved, as well as a reduction in the time spent mentoring inexperienced CBD developers. Even greater benefits can be obtained from tools that allow you to tailor the Select Perspective (or alternative SMaC CBD process) to your particular organizations needs and learn from the experience gained over time.

Many well-known process communication tools, such as Rational's RUP, are both restricted to object-oriented legacy processes and are not suitable for process modification and improvement. Select Process Director is the primary delivery tool for Select Perspective. It allows you to configure the core process to your organization's needs, and then generate Microsoft Project plans and records progress against the activities. It also stores the project metrics, and this historical project information can then be used to estimate future projects or processes.

In summary, many tools are actually available to help to automate component- and service-based development. It is not usually worth bending the current tools or reinventing wheels. Experience shows that using these tools increases the quality of the application as well as increasing productivity and reducing costs. When implemented smoothly and efficiently, Select Perspective's SMaC enables these benefits through aggregation/simplification, parallel development, plug-and-play maintenance and component/service reuse.

More detail on these types of tools and other related component- and service-based development tools can also be found in the full version of Select Perspective, which is delivered in Aonix Select Business Solution's Select Process Director (www.selectbs.com).

Epilogue: taking it on 12

Whether you read this book in the office, at home or on a beach vacation in the south of France, we hope you found the ideas useful. If you are new to component- and service-based development, you should now have a reasonable understanding of the underlying concepts and feel ready to embark on those first few projects. While defining Select Perspective, we made many mistakes along the way, and you probably will too. As they say, 'you can never learn everything from the mistakes of others'. We wish you all the best in your endeavors.

Many areas may have been familiar to those of you already building component- and service-based systems. This book should assist you in evolving your own ideas and the approach you take on CBD projects in the future. As component- and service-based development is becoming more and more pervasive, this real-world experience with templates for roles, deliverables and processes should help to reinforce your existing best practices. You are not alone in the development of component- and service-based applications; we empathize and offer you our support.

Experienced Select Perspective practitioners will also have found new insights and experience-based updates. Select Perspective has evolved significantly, but the core values and concepts still remain. This commitment to the development of Select Perspective keeps it alive and contemporary, and we thank all of you who have helped along the way. This said, this is not the end and Select Perspective will continue to advance. Just as Select Perspective merged OMT, use case modeling, BPM and data modeling in the early days, mapped to OO UML and then on to component- and service-based development, it has the capability to be continuously current.

Once again, this book represents our latest thinking and evolution of Select Perspective. You will have seen the three key principles of Select Perspective:

1 small set of key deliverables (pragmatic);

2 based on experience (proven);

3 designed to fit most organizations (adaptive);

These principles make Select Perspective fit for real-world solution delivery. You should also have grasped the overarching concept of supply, manage and consume (SMaC), which maps back to many other engineering disciplines. If there is one concept from Select Perspective that you should take with you from this book, it is that of 'supply, manage and consume'.

If you implement some, or all of Select Perspective, you will find that it is invaluable for CIOs, IT directors, project managers, analysts, and solution designers and developers who need a contemporary software development process. It meets the many demands of modern solution delivery. Select Perspective is a comprehensive development life cycle for component-based solutions that supports business-aligned parallel development in order to reduce time-to-market.

Select Perspective provides technical, business, and economic benefits. Technically, the simplification through 'abstraction' and 'containment of complexity' makes life a lot easier. Massive parallel development and the capability to outsource development results in faster development cycles – you simply get there quicker, giving significant business benefits. Delegating components and services means that we do not all have to become experts in things that are not related directly to our business. Finally, and most importantly, economic benefits come from Select Perspective's component and service reuse and pluggable maintenance. These benefits stem from;

- abstraction and simplification;
- design-by-contract parallel development;
- pluggable maintenance;
- component and service reuse.

The future is never certain, but Select Perspective's track record has shown it to be highly suited to continuous evolution. As technologies evolve rapidly, the underlying concepts of SMaC, iteration, business alignment, pragmatism, flexibility and real-world experience have remained fairly constant. This means that Select Perspective is well positioned to take on the technologies and architectures of tomorrow, whatever they may be.

We have said this many times before in this book, but this is the last time. This book represents a small subset of the full Select Perspective, which is documented in Select Process Director. If you want to dig deeper or have further questions, please contact any of the authors, or Aonix Select Business Solutions.

'Happy component- and service-based development.'

Glossary

Note: In the following descriptions, 'OMG-UML V1.x' indicates a formal definition from the Unified Modeling Language (UML) standard.

Activity. A generic term used to describe a process group, process thread, or elementary business process.

Actor. A role (or set of roles) that is played in relation to a delivered solution; it could be a person, a group of persons, an organization, another system or a piece of equipment. An actor can be external or internal to the business, for example customer or credit controller. An actor can be considered a role that has a specific set of responsibilities relating to a set of use cases.

Aggregation. A whole/part relationship where the whole or aggregate is composed of one or more elements (components, classes), each of which is considered a part of the aggregate.

Architecture. 'The organizational structure and associated behavior of a system. An architecture can be recursively decomposed into parts that interact through interfaces, relationships that connect then parts, and constraints for assembling parts. Parts that interact through interfaces include classes, components, and subsystems'. [OMG-UML V1.x]

Argument. The actual value of a parameter.

Association. A semantic relationship between two or more interfaces, components, classes, or data types that specifies connections between their instances.

Attribute. A named property of a class that describes a range of values that instances can hold.

Behavior. 'The observable effects of an operation or event, including its results'. [OMG-UML V1.x]

Behavior model. 'A model aspect that emphasizes the behavior of the instances in a system, including their methods, collaborations, and state histories'. [OMG-UML V1.x]

BPI. Business process improvement.

BPM. Business process modeling.

BPR. Business process re-engineering.

Business actor. A role that has a specific set of responsibilities relating to a business process. A business actor can be external, internal or system, for example customer, credit controller, credit control system.

Business component. A kind of component that contains business logic and data.

Business event. A stimulus that triggers an activity; it may be input- or output-driven. Input-driven business events are signaled by the arrival of an input information flow. Output-driven business events may be temporal or conditional. Temporal events are signaled by the arrival of a predefined point in time. Conditional events report the sensing of a particular circumstance that triggers an activity, for example credit limit exceeded.

Business process. A collection of activities that takes in one or more kinds of input and creates an output that is of value to the customer.

Business process improvement (BPI). Under some circumstances, the radical nature of the changes envisaged with a BPR exercise are unacceptable, resulting in a drive for improvement of the current processes, however defined, rather than re-engineering. The term 'BPI' is used to indicate where improvements are sought within the current business constraints.

Business process re-engineering (BPR). The radical reorganization of an enterprise along the flow of work that generates the value sought by the customer.

Business rule. A rule defines the actions that need to occur in a business when a particular situation arises. Business rules assert a policy or structure of a business, or control or influence the behavior of the business. A business rule is broken down into an event that triggers a rule with test conditions that result in defined actions.

Change request. A modification to a software solution thought to be necessary by the client, business users, or developers.

Class. 'A description of a set of objects that share the same attributes, operations, methods, relationships, and semantics'. [OMG-UML V1.x]

Class diagram. 'A diagram that shows a collection of declarative (static) model elements, such as classes, types, and their content and relationships'. [OMG-UML V1.x]

Client. 1. The economic buyer of the results of a development project. 2. A software element, such as a component, that requests a service from another software element.

Collaboration diagram. A diagram that shows interactions organized around the structure of a model, using either interfaces, components, classes and associations, or instances and links. Unlike a sequence diagram, a collaboration diagram shows the relationships between instances. This is particularly suited to providing a view of the interactions required to service a use case scenario. See *Sequence diagram.*

Component. A unit of software that conforms to a component model, and can be deployed, and composed independently without modification according to a composition standard. Software entities interact with a component using the component's clearly defined interfaces; an interaction standard defines the elements of the interface.

Component diagram. 'A diagram that shows the organizations and dependencies among components'. [OMG-UML V1.x]

Component library. A repository of pre-existing components.

Component model. A model aspect that defines the structure of the parts of a component, including the behavior of instances in a component, including their methods, collaborations, and state histories.

Configuration management. Procedures that define the process of building a version of a software element such as a component or solution from its constituent program and data files.

Consumer. Uses a pre-existing component to deploy it for use within a software solution or system. The consumer may be another developer an IT department, or an independent software vendor. See *Suppliers*.

Context diagram. A simplified diagram that is useful for specifying the boundaries and scope of a system.

Contract. The list of requests, with associated operation signatures, that a component can make of another component. Under the design by contract theory, a software system is viewed as a set of communicating components whose interaction is based on precisely defined specifications of the mutual obligations: contracts.

Controller. An object whose responsibility is to coordinate several different components or objects. Typical kinds of controller are the user interface controller, which is responsible for the elements of a screen layout, and the process controller, which is responsible for use case coordination.

Coupling. Defines how closely linked different software elements are, e.g. components or objects. Loose coupling means that the elements pass only minimal information between them and do not share data and program code. Close-coupled systems are highly dependent on each other.

Datatype. 'A descriptor of a set of values that lack identity and whose operations do not have side effects. Datatypes include primitive pre-defined types and user-definable types. Pre-defined types include numbers, string, and time. User-definable types include enumerations'. [OMG-UML V1.x]

Data dictionary. A repository that is used to store the details of the entities of the database. It will define tables, relations, and field details, which are sometimes referred to as meta-data or 'data about data'.

Data migration. The transfer of data from one system to another, often newer, system. When data are added to a database, this is known as 'populating the database'.

Data component. Data components provide infrastructure for the storage and retrieval of entities in a data management system (for example a DBMS or file system). Data components insulate other components from the effects of changes in technology by isolating data management system (DBMS) dependencies.

Dependency. 'A relationship between two modeling elements, in which a change in one modeling element (the independent element) will affect the other modeling element (the dependent element)'. [OMG-UML V1.x]

Deployment diagram. 'A diagram that shows the configuration of run-time processing nodes and the components, processes, and objects that live on them. Components represent run-time manifestations of code units'. [OMG-UML V1.x]

Domain. 'An area of knowledge or activity characterized by a set of concepts and terminology understood by the practitioners in that area'. [OMG-UML V1.x]

Domain model. A collection of artifacts – business process model, information model, business rules, and constraints – used to define the requirements for a solution.

Element. 'An atomic constituent of a model'. [OMG-UML V1.x]

Elementary business process (*EBP*). A task that is performed in response to a business event by one person in one place at one time, that adds measurable business value to the customer and leaves the data in a consistent state; for example approve credit or price order. Elementary business processes can be reused both within and across different process threads.

Event. 'The specification of a significant occurrence that has a location in time and space. In the context of state diagrams, an event is an occurrence that can trigger a transition'. [OMG-UML V1.x]

External object (*class*). An external object provides a reference to an object in a separate work space. Static associations may then be drawn from a class within a project to the external class (shown as a double-lined box on a class diagram). Messages can similarly be sent to the external object using a collaboration diagram or sequence diagram.

Framework. '1. A stereotype package consisting mainly of patterns. 2. An architectural pattern that provides an extensible template for applications within a specific domain'. [OMG-UML V1.x]

Functional requirement. A statement of what the system is expected to do, irrespective of non-functional requirements.

Generalization. 'A taxonomic relationship between a more general element and a more specific element. The more specific element is fully consistent with the more general element and contains more additional information. An instance of the more specific element may be used where the more general element is allowed. See *Inheritance*'. [OMG-UML V1.x]

Guideline. A document that provides a set of instructions, tips, and tricks to assist in a specific domain or development activity, such as user interface guidelines.

Human–computer interface (*HCI*). The interface between users of a system and the system itself.

Implementation. 'A definition of how something is constructed or computed. For example, a class is an implementation of a type, a method is an implementation of an operation'. [OMG-UML V1.x]

Implementation constraint. A non-functional requirement that specifies how the system is to be implemented, for example use of specified operating system and DBMS.

Infrastructure. The basic structural foundations of a system; includes operating system, communications software, database management software, and HCI software.

Inheritance. 'The mechanism by which more specific elements incorporate structure and behavior of more general elements related by behavior'. [OMG-UML V1.x]

Instance. 'An entity to which a set of operations can be applied and which has a state that stores the effects of the operations. See *Object*'. [OMG-UML V1.x]

Integrated development environment (IDE). A system for supporting the process of writing software. Such a system may include a syntax-directed editor, graphical tools for program entry, and integrated support for compiling and running the program and relating compilation errors back to the source code.

Interface. An interface is an abstraction of the behavior of a component that consists of a subset of the interactions of that component together with a set of constraints describing when they occur. The interfaces of a component form a partition of the interactions of that component; thus, an interface constitutes the part of the component's behavior that is obtained by considering only the interactions of that interface and hiding all other interactions.

Joint application design (JAD). A structured approach to the use of group dynamics in systems development that is particularly useful in requirements capture and user interface modeling.

Legacy asset. A software product, developed on the basis of older technologies, that is so vital to an enterprise that it cannot be replaced or disrupted without a major impact on the enterprise. Legacy assets come in various forms: function libraries, programs, program fragments, data structures, database interfaces, data models, etc.

Legacy system. When a new computer-based solution is developed, it may be necessary to retain hardware – but more often software – from the earlier system. In these cases, the software that has been retained is referred to as a 'legacy system'. See *Legacy asset.*

Message. 'A specification of the conveyance of information from one instance to another, with the expectation that activity will ensue. A message may specify that raising of a signal or the call of an operation'. [OMG-UML V1.x]

Method. 'The implementation of an operation. It specifies the algorithm or procedure associated with an operation'. [OMG-UML V1.x]

Metric. A measure of software quality that indicates the complexity, understandability, testability, description, and intricacy of code.

Middleware. A type of software that acts as a layer between other software to assist in data transfer between incompatible parts.

Model. 'An abstraction of a physical system, with a certain purpose'. [OMG-UML V1.x]

Model element. 'An element that is an abstraction drawn from the system being modeled'. [OMG-UML V1.x]

Module. 'A software unit of storage and manipulation. Modules include source code modules, binary code modules, and executable code modules. See *Component*'. [OMG-UML V1.x]

Non-functional requirement. A statement of how a system is to be implemented or how well the system is expected to function. Examples of 'how' include proposed hardware configurations and software infrastructure. Examples of 'how well' include reliability, efficiency, usability, maintainability, testability, portability and reusability.

Node. A node represents a runtime computational resource that generally has at least a memory and often computational capability. Runtime objects and components may reside on nodes.

Object. 'An entity with a well-defined boundary and identity that encapsulates state and behavior. State is represented by attributes and relationships; behavior is represented by operations, methods, and state machines. An object is an instance of a class. See *Class, Instance*'. [OMG-UML V1.x]

Object diagram. 'A diagram that encompasses objects and their relationships at a point in time. An object diagram may be considered a special case of a class diagram or a collaboration diagram'. [OMG-UML V1.x]

Operation. 'A service that can be requested from an object to effect behavior. An operation has a signature, which may restrict the actual parameters that are possible'. [OMG-UML V1.x]

Package. 'A general-purpose mechanism for organizing elements into groups. Packages can be nested within other packages'. [OMG-UML V1.x]

Parameter. 'The specification of a variable that can be changed, passed, or returned. A parameter may include a name, type, and direction. Parameters are used for operations, messages, and events'. [OMG-UML V1.x]

Pattern. A pattern consists of a three-part rule, which expresses a relation between a certain context, a certain system of forces (problems) that occurs repeatedly in that context, and a certain software configuration that allows these forces to resolve themselves (solution). Succinctly, a pattern is a proven solution to a problem in a context.

Persistent data model. The organization of data into records or tables according to DBMS architectural constraints but independently of physical characteristics.

Post-condition. 'A constraint that must be true at the completion of an operation'. [OMG-UML V1.x]

Precondition. 'A constraint that must be true when an operation is invoked'. [OMG-UML V1.x].

Process. '1. A heavyweight unit of concurrency and execution in an operating system. 2. A software development process – the steps and guidelines by which to develop a system. 3. To execute an algorithm or otherwise handle something dynamically'. [OMG-UML V1.x]

Process group. A grouping of one or more related process threads.

Process hierarchy diagram. A diagram that shows the hierarchical structure of business processes.

Process thread. A sequence of business activities initiated by a business event that produces a result that represents business value. A result from one process thread is often a business event relative to another process thread. Process threads can be clustered into process groups.

Process thread diagram. A diagram showing the events, activity sequence, and results with the relationships between them.

Prototype. A preliminary version of part or a framework of all of a solution that can be reviewed by end-users.

Provisioning. The activities associated with locating possible components for reuse, which may involve payments to third-party suppliers.

Quality attribute. A non-functional requirement that specifies 'how well' the system is expected to function, for example performance, reliability and usability.

Refinement. 'A relationship that represent a fuller specification of something that has already been specified at a certain level of detail'. [OMG-UML V1.x]

Release. A release is a version of a piece of software that has been made public (as opposed to a version that is in development, or otherwise unreleased.) A release is either a major release, a revision, or a 'bug fix'.

Repository. A facility for storing models, interfaces, and implementations.

Requirement. 'A desired feature, property, or behavior of a system'. [OMG-UML V1.x]

Reuse. 'The use of a pre-existing artifact'. [OMG-UML V1.x]

Role. 'The named specific behavior of an entity participating in a particular context. A role may be static (e.g. an association end) or dynamic (e.g. a collaboration role)'. [OMG-UML V1.x]

Scenario. 'A specific sequence of actions that illustrate behavior. A scenario may be used to illustrate an interaction or execution of a use case instance'. [OMG-UML V1.x]

Sequence diagram. 'A diagram that shows object interactions arranged in time sequence. In particular it shows the objects participating in the interaction and the sequence of messages exchanged. A sequence diagram can exist in a generic form (describes all possible scenarios) and in instance form (describes one actual scenario)'. [OMG-UML V1.x]

Service. A publicly exposed capability (function) of a software application, e.g. web service, that provides a platform-neutral execution capability for other software solutions to use the service.

Service class. A type of class providing one or more services that realizes a component interface(s.)

Signature. 'The named parameters of a behavioral feature. A signature may include an operational returned parameter'. [OMG-UML V1.x]

Solution delivery. Solution delivery is the development process that realizes the architecture of the application in terms of its business components, and user classes within a technical framework. This is a view of the solution based on concepts that are meaningful to the developers and programmers. It may require the production of a user interface prototype that increases understanding of a business or technology issue, which in turn reduces the risk associated with the solution.

Standard. An established measure of comparison. This term includes propriety vendor and producer standards, as well as national and international standards produced by recognized standards bodies.

State. 'A condition or situation during the life of an object during which it satisfies some condition, performs some action, or waits for some event'. [OMG-UML V1.x]

State diagram. A diagram that shows the sequences of states that an object or an interaction goes through during its life in response to events, together with its responses and actions.

Stereotype. 'A new type of modeling element that extends the semantics of the metamodel. Stereotypes must be based on certain existing types or classes in the metamodel. Stereotypes may extend the semantics, but not the structure of pre-existing types and classes. Certain stereotypes are defined in UML; others may be user defined'. [OMG-UML V1.x]

Subclass. 'In a generalization relationship, the specialization of another class: the superclass. See *Generalization*'. [OMG-UML V1.x]

Superclass. 'In a generalization relationship, the generalization of another class: the subclass. See *Generalization*'. [OMG-UML V1.x]

Supplier. A supplier develops and offers components for distribution to interested consumers. Suppliers may provide components for retail sale, as open-source software, or as free software. See *Consumers*.

Thin client. In a network system, this describes an architecture where the bulk of the processing is carried out on a central server, e.g. web host.

Three-tier client/server. The client is mainly used for display, with application logic and business rules partitioned on a second-tier server and a third-tier database server. Here the client is sometimes referred to as a 'thin client', because the size of the executable software is smaller.

Use case. 'The specification of a sequence of actions, including variants, that a system (or other entity) can perform, interacting with actors of the system'. [OMG-UML V1.x]

Use case diagram. 'A diagram that shows the relationships among actors and use cases within the system'. [OMG-UML V1.x]

Use case model. 'A model that describes a system's functional requirements in terms of use cases'. [OMG-UML V1.x]

View. 'A projection of a model, which is seen from a given perspective or vantage point and omits entities that are not relevant to this perspective'. [OMG-UML V1.x]

Wrapper. A component that provides a message-based interface to non-object-oriented software, such as legacy assets.

References

Allen, P., and Frost, S. (1998) *Component-Based Development for Enterprise Systems, Applying the Select Perspective*, SIGS Books and Cambridge University Press.

Beck, K. (2000) *Extreme Programming Explained, Embracing Change*, Addison-Wesley.

Beck, K., and Cunningham, W. (1989) 'A laboratory for teaching object oriented thinking', Proceedings of OOPSLA'89 (1–6).

Bellows, J. (2000) 'Activity diagrams and operation architecture', On-line at www.cbd-hq.com/articles/2000/000201jb_activitydiagrams.asp.

Bocij, P., Chaffey, D., Greasley, A., and Hickie, S. (1999) *Business Information Systems; Technology, Development and Management*, Pitman Publishing.

D'Souza, D.F., and Wills, A.C. (1999) *Objects, Components, and Frameworks with UML: The Catalysis Approach*, Addison-Wesley.

Eles, P., and Sims, O. (1998) *Building Business Objects*, John Wiley & Sons.

Fowler, M. (1999) *Refactoring: Improving the Design of Existing Code*, Addison-Wesley.

Gamma, E., Helm, R., Johnson, R., and Vlissides, J. (1994) *Design Patterns: Elements of Reusable Object Oriented Software*, Addison-Wesley.

Heineman, G., and Council, W. (2001) *Component-based Software Engineering: Putting the Pieces Together*, Addison-Wesley.

Jacobson, I. (1994) *The Object Advantage. Business Process Reengineering with Object Technology*, Addison-Wesley.

Meyer, B. (1997) *Object-Oriented Software Construction* (2nd edn), Prentice Hall.

Rumbaugh, J., Blaha, M., Premarlain, W., Eddy, F., and Lorensen, B. (1990) *Object-oriented Modeling and Design*, Prentice Hall.

Further reading

Ambler, S. (1998) *Process Patterns: Building Large Scale Systems Using Object Technology*, Cambridge University Press.

Alexander, C. (1977) *Pattern Language: Towns, Buildings Construction*, Oxford University Press.

Ambler, S. (1999) *More Process Patterns: Building Large Scale Systems Using Object Technology*, Cambridge University Press.

Booch, G., Rumbaugh, J., and Jacobson, I. (1999) *The Unified Modeling Language User Guide*, Addison-Wesley.

Fowler, M. (2000) *UML Distilled* (2nd edn), Addison-Wesley.

Jaaksi, A. *et al.* (1999) *Tried & True Object Development*, Cambridge University Press.

Jacobson, I. (1995) *The Object Advantage: BPR with Object Technology*, Addison-Wesley.

Karlsson, E.A. (1995) *Software Reuse, A Holistic Approach*, John Wiley & Sons.

Kruchten, P. (1999) *The Rational Unified Process, An Introduction*, Addison-Wesley.

McGibbon, B. (1995) *Managing Your Move to Object Technology*, SIGS Books.

Taylor, D.A. (1995) *Business Engineering with Object Technology*, John Wiley & Sons.

Wirfs-Brock, R., Wilkerson, B., and Wiener, L. (1990) *Designing Object Oriented Software*, Prentice Hall.

Select Cruises

Select Cruises

Select Cruises provides sailing adventure holidays on tall ships as working members of the crew. Tall ships are based in New Zealand and the Caribbean, from where they undertake both long and short sail passages from their home base. These cruises consist of 'legs' from island to island, e.g. Auckland to Tonga, Tonga to Vava'u, Vava'u to Western Samoa, and berths may be purchased for one or more legs of a cruise. Each tall ship has a maximum of twenty-four berths available for guests in addition to the twelve for the professional crew. Different types of berth, such as bunk, hammock, in cabin, and in dormitory, can be requested by guests. Computer support is needed to handle sales enquiries and berth bookings.

Sales enquiries come from a number of sources: direct calls, responses to adverts (postal), and on-line enquiries through the new website. Contact with prospective customers requires access to the cruise schedule and berth availability, as well as the database of existing customers; all new customers are added to this list. Every enquiry is logged, so that sales performance and activity can be analyzed to help with future cruise planning.

When cruise reservations are made, a letter of confirmation – a quote – is sent detailing the cruise passages, dates, costs, etc.; these reservations are valid for only one month. This quote is recorded and can then be recalled when the customer confirms the booking. Bookings mean that payment is made against the customer's credit card and the reservation becomes confirmed. (See Figure A2.)

Note

The following detail are *partial* extracts from the Select Cruises case study; complete examples can be found on www.selectbs.com.

Business alignment workflow

Business process model

The development of the application begins with the business process modeling within the business alignment workflow. The following is a complete process hierarchy and process thread diagram model for Select Cruises (Figures A1, A2, A3 and A4).

Figure A1
Select Cruises

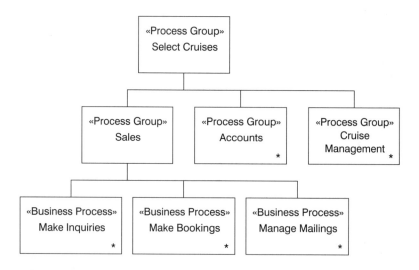

Business process: Make Inquiries

Objective
To provide prospective customers with information on scheduled cruises, berth availability, and costs through different communication channels.

Description
Staff deal with telephone inquiries regarding brochures, cruises, available berths, and costs, which may then be passed to Bookings if the customer chooses a cruise.

Prospects may also examine cruise information and berth availability through the website. Requests for brochures and booking forms can be made through e-forms on the site. On-line booking is not available.

Business process: Make Bookings

Objective

To make bookings for berths for customers on scheduled cruises.

Description

Tele-sales uses the booking form to collect and record the customer's details, select the possible cruise options and confirm berth availability, with the costs. Discuss the options with customer and suggest alternatives if selections not accepted. When accepted, collect credit card details, record the reservations, and tell customer their booking reference. Print confirmation letter and pass details to Accounts for collecting deposit.

For postal sales, use the booking forms to record customer details and select chosen cruises, then check berth availability. If request can be fulfilled, make the reservations, enter credit card details for deposit, print confirmation letter for customer and pass to Accounts for processing deposit. If customer request cannot be met, select alternative options and pass details to Tele-sales.

Business process: Manage Mailings

Objective

To send brochures and letters to prospects and customers.

Description

Accept instructions from Inquiries and Bookings to send brochures or letters to prospects or customers and record date of posting.

Elementary business process: Record Prospect's Details

Description

Captures and records the details of a new customer or retrieves the details of an existing customer member. If the request is for a brochure only, then this completes the inquiry.

Elementary business process: Record Cruise Preferences

Description

Records the customer's preferences for the kind of cruise required, e.g. ocean, time of year, budget, which are then used to select cruises to match these preferences.

Elementary business process: Search Cruises

Description

Finds cruises to match customer's preferences.

Figure A2
Make
Inquiries

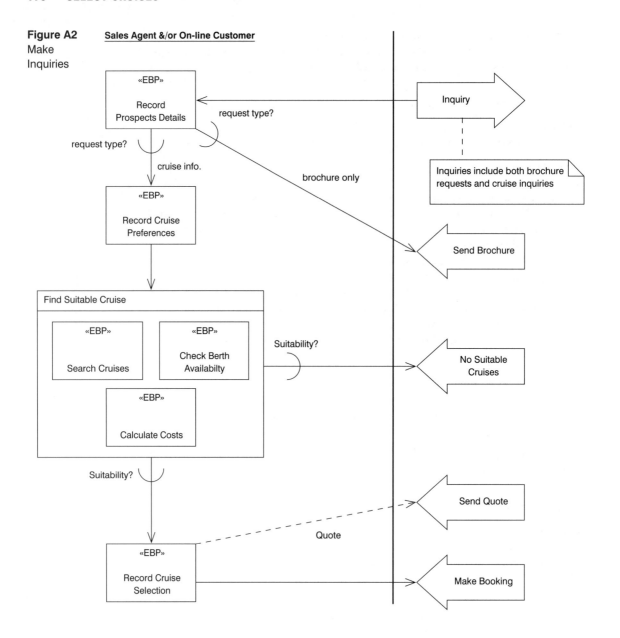

Elementary business process: Check Berth Availability

Description
Checks if berths are still available on the chosen cruise dates.

Elementary business process: Calculate Costs

Description

Calculates the cost of the cruise based on chosen cruise passages and dates.

Elementary business process: Record Cruise Selection

Description

If cruise matches customer's requirements then records the selection and either
sends a written quote or moves to make a booking.

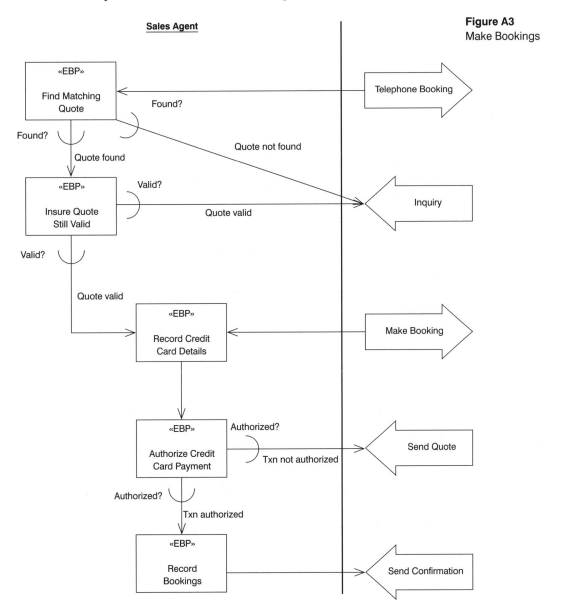

Figure A3
Make Bookings

Elementary business process: Find Matching Quote

Description

Uses a quote reference provided by the caller to find the matching quote. If no quote found, then treats as a new inquiry.

Elementary business process: Insure Quote Still Valid

Description

If the quote found, then checks that berths are still available on that cruise. If quote still valid, moves to confirm the booking, otherwise tries to find alternative cruise dates.

Elementary business process: Record Credit Card Details

Description

Captures the customer's credit card details.

Elementary business process: Authorize Credit Card Payment

Description

Based on the cruise costs, takes a payment from the credit card using the on-line service. If authorization fails, then sends a quote with details of payment, otherwise records the sale.

Elementary business process: Record Bookings

Description

Confirms the cruise bookings and sends confirmation.

Elementary business process: Print Customer Quotation

Description

Prints appropriate letter to customer.

Elementary business process: Print Customer Confirmation

Description

Prints appropriate letter to customer.

Elementary business process: Print Brochure Letter

Description

Prints appropriate letter to customer.

Manage Mailings

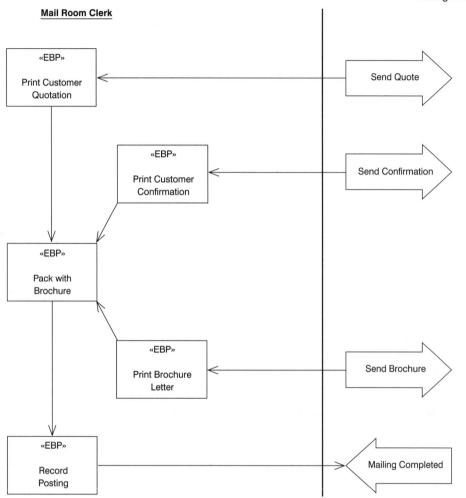

Elementary business process: Pack with Brochure

Description

Makes up a mailing package to include the brochure.

Elementary business process: Record Posting

Description

Records that the mailing has been sent.

Use case model

Within business alignment, the business process models cover both intended automated processes and manual ones. The UML use case model defines the system requirements for the automated processes and explicitly scopes the functionality of the intended solutions.

The following use case model (Figure A5) describes the scoped functional requirements of the Select Cruises solution, derived from the business process model.

Figure A5
Sales

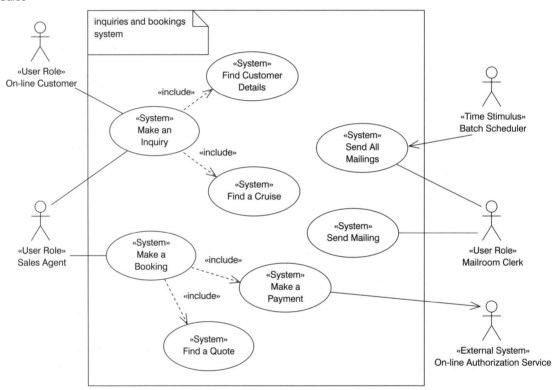

Use case: Make a Booking

Intent

To confirm a customer's reservation for cruises that may be the result of a previous quote. Also take credit card payment for the booking.

Description

System includes Find a Quote.

Actor confirms quote reservation.

System includes Make a Payment.

Actor confirms bookings are paid.

System records bookings.

System requests confirmation mailing.

Pre_conditions: cruise information available.

Post_conditions: booking reservations confirmed; confirmation mailing requested.

Alternate_courses: payment refused: send a quote; quote not found or invalid: use Make an Inquiry.

Use case: Send Mailing

Intent

To print and record the sending of letters and brochures to prospects and customers.

Description

System presents list of mailings.

Actor selects mailing(s) to send.

System prints appropriate letter to customer.

System records date of mailing.

Pre_conditions: letter text available.

Post_conditions: mailing date recorded.

Alternate_courses: none.

Use case: Find a Quote

Intent

To check if an issued quote for berths on a cruise for a customer is still valid, i.e. berths still available.

Description

Actor enters quote reference.

System locates quote record.

Actor confirms quote.

System verifies reservations still available.

Pre_conditions: cruise information available.

Post_conditions: none.

Alternate_courses: quote not found: use Make an Inquiry.

Use case: Make a Payment

Intent

To collect customer's credit card details and charge card for payment.

Description

System displays credit card form.

Actor enters credit card details.

System verifies entered credit card details.

Actor confirms payment amount.

System uses on-line authorization service.

System displays result of authorization.

Actor confirms result.

Pre_conditions: authorization service available.

Post_conditions: payment recorded.

Alternate_courses: none.

Use case: Find a Cruise

Intent

To search for cruises according to specified criteria, to show berth types and availability, and to calculate costs.

Description

System presents choices of cruises.

Actor selects cruise.

System presents passages on selected cruise.

Actor selects passage.

System presents berth details on passage.

Actor selects berth(s).

System displays costs of cruise.

Actor confirms selections.

Pre_conditions: cruise details available.

Post_conditions: cruise selection confirmed.

Alternate_courses: searching abandoned.

Use case: Make an Inquiry

Intent

To provide prospective customers with information on scheduled cruises, berth availability and costs through a tele-sales agent or via on-line web pages. Also used for postal bookings and lost/expired quotes for reservations.

Description

System includes Record Customer Details.

System includes Find A Cruise.

Actor chooses to have a quote or make a booking.

System records quote and displays reference.

Actor confirms quote reference.

System requests quote mailing.

Pre_conditions: scheduled cruises available.

Post_conditions: detail of enquiry/quote recorded; mailing request recorded.

Alternate_courses: no suitable cruise found: detail recorded; quote not necessary: use Make a Booking; brochure only requested: record brochure mailing request.

Use case: Find Customer Details

Intent

To retrieve or collect customer's contact details, sailing ability, and cruise preferences.

Description

Actor chooses new or existing customer options.

For existing customers:
   actor enters customer reference;
   system locates customer record and displays details;
   actor confirms the details.

For new customers:
   actor enters personal details (name, address, etc.);
   system displays cruise choices;
   actor selects cruise preferences;
   actor confirms the details;
   system records customer details.

Pre_conditions: none

Post_conditions: customer details recorded

Alternate_courses: existing customer records not found; new customer detail entry abandoned.

Use case: Send All Mailings

Intent

To provide a 'batch' process to send all letters.

Description

System retrieves list of mailings.

System prints appropriate letter to each customer.

System records date of mailing for each letter printed.

Pre_conditions: none.

Post_conditions: date of mailing recorded.

Alternate_courses: none.

Business architecture models

Figure A6
Business
Architecture

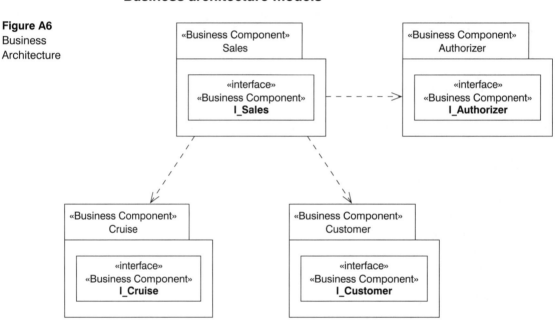

The diagram (Figure A6) shows the initial component map after the component chunking exercise, packages are added to represent the logical components, and each component has an interface added to discover its services during the interaction modeling.

Component interaction modeling

Each of the use cases has its child object sequence diagram, which defines the component services and the component interactions. Note from the following diagrams (Figures A7–A13) that a use case controller (or process control) object has been added to manage the business process flow of the use case and the interactions with the collaborating business components.

Figure A7
Requirements: Make an Inquiry

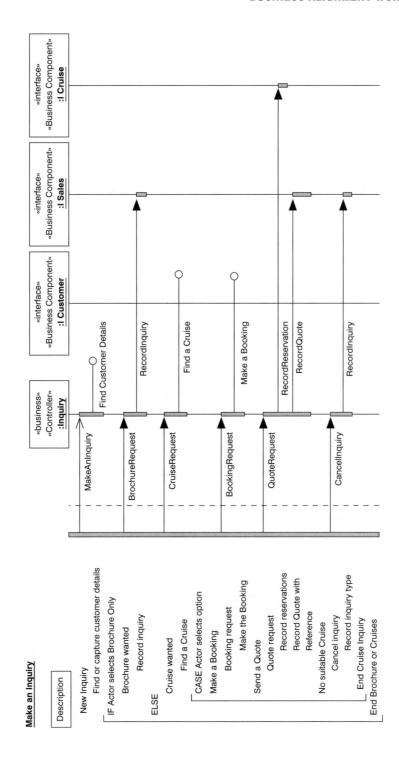

Make an Inquiry

Description

New Inquiry
  Find or capture customer details
IF Actor selects Brochure Only
  Brochure wanted
    Record inquiry
ELSE
  Cruise wanted
    Find a Cruise
    CASE Actor selects option
    Make a Booking
      Booking request
      Make the Booking
    Send a Quote
      Quote request
        Record reservations
        Record Quote with
          Reference
    No suitable Cruise
      Cancel inquiry
        Record inquiry type
    End Cruise Inquiry
End Brochure or Cruises

Figure A8
Requirements: Find Customer Details

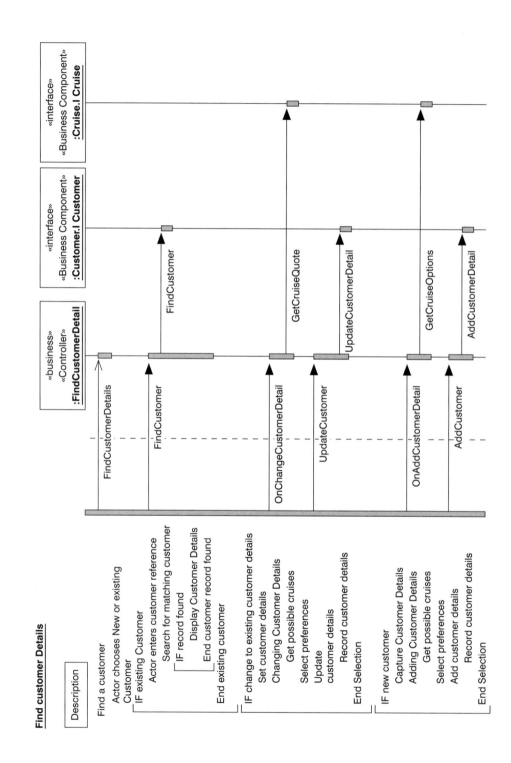

Find customer Details

Figure A9
Requirements: Find a Cruise

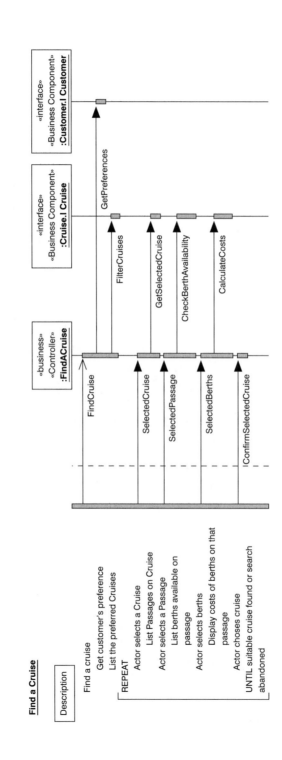

Figure A10
Requirements: Make a Booking

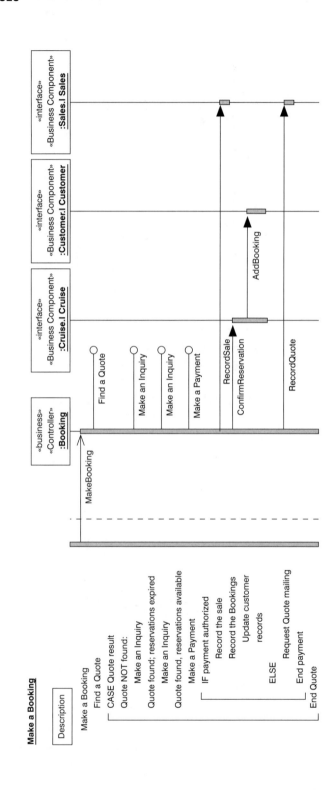

<u>**Make a Booking**</u>

Description

Make a Booking
    Find a Quote
    CASE Quote result
        Quote NOT found:
            Make an Inquiry
        Quote found; reservations expired
            Make an Inquiry
        Quote found, reservations available
            Make a Payment
            IF payment authorized
                Record the sale
                Record the Bookings
                Update customer
                    records
            ELSE
                Request Quote mailing
            End payment
    End Quote

Figure A11
Requirements: Make a Payment

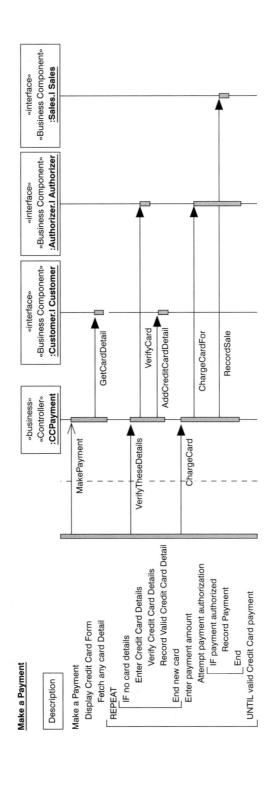

Make a Payment

Description

Make a Payment
  Display Credit Card Form
  Fetch any card Detail
  REPEAT
    IF no card details
      Enter Credit Card Details
      Verify Credit Card Details
      Record Valid Credit Card Detail
    End new card
    Enter payment amount
    Attempt payment authorization
    IF payment authorized
      Record Payment
    End
  UNTIL valid Credit Card payment

Figure A12
Requirements: Find a Quote

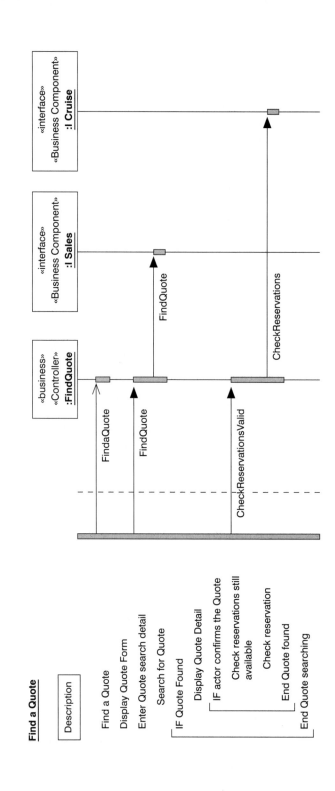

Find a Quote

Description

Find a Quote
Display Quote Form
Enter Quote search detail
Search for Quote
IF Quote Found
Display Quote Detail
IF actor confirms the Quote
Check reservations still available
Check reservation
End Quote found
End Quote searching

Send Mailing

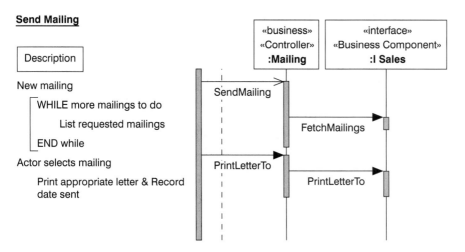

Information model

The information model for the solution is also developed, initially as a class diagram, then migrated to a first-cut logical data model.

Component and solution delivery

Following on from the alignment and architecture definitions, under supply, manage and consume, we have the solution (consume) and the component (supply) delivery workflows. Solution delivery concerns itself with the design of the user interface and integration of the business services to create the solution. Component delivery concerns itself with the design and implementation of the business components. Both are constrained by the technical architecture definition. The following diagrams show a part of the technical architecture required to deliver the Select Cruises solution, then diagrams showing the design/implementation techniques used in support of the supply–consume delivery relationship follow these.

Technical architecture

The following is an extract from the technical architecture definition:

 User interface controllers will be incorporated into the design and implementation of the solution, responsible for managing the page navigation sequence and delegating business service calls to process controllers. The page sequence will be data-driven. The technical architecture provides an extensible (by inheritance) interface controller component and the ability to specify and load data to drive the navigation. The following diagrams (Figures A14–A20) illustrate the component, its extension mechanism and pattern of use.

Figure A14
Information Model (cruise)

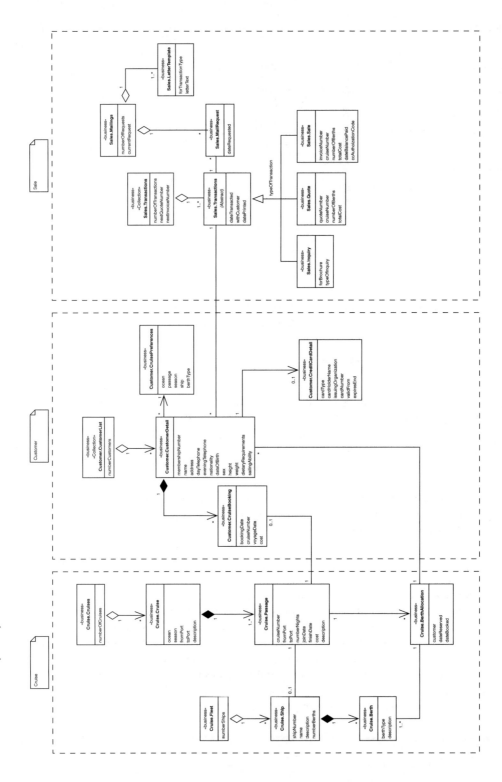

Figure A15
First-cut Data Schema (sales)

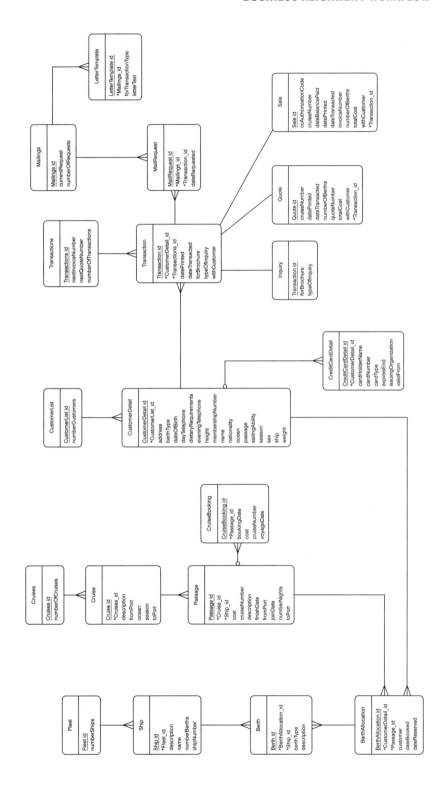

Figure A16
TechArch: interface controller design/reuse

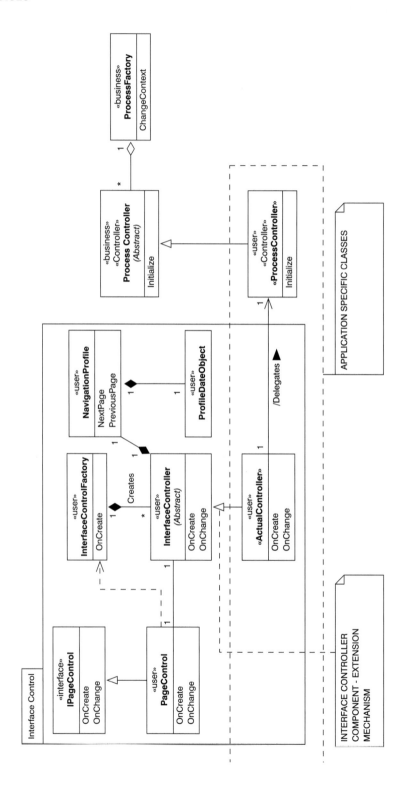

Figure A17
TechArch: controller pattern

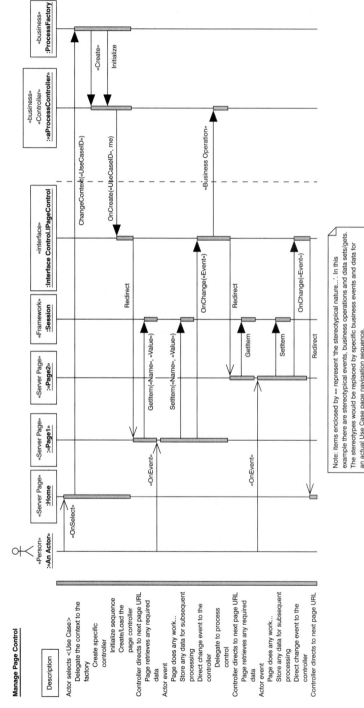

Figure A18
TechArch: page sequence specification

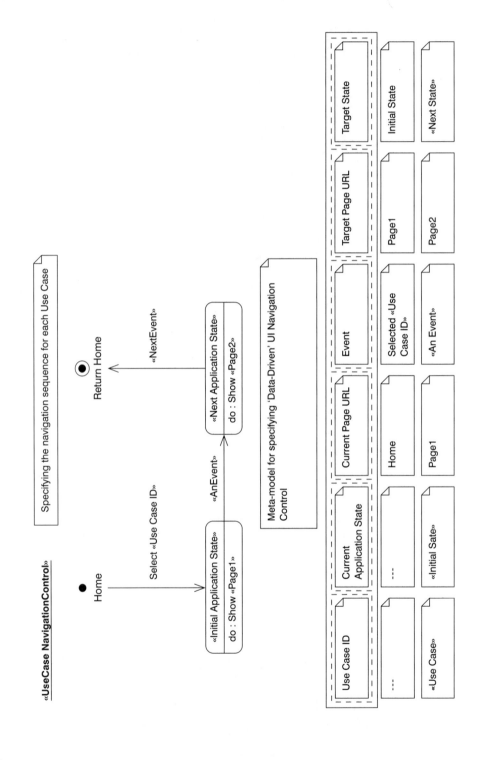

Figure A19
TechArch: inheritance controllers

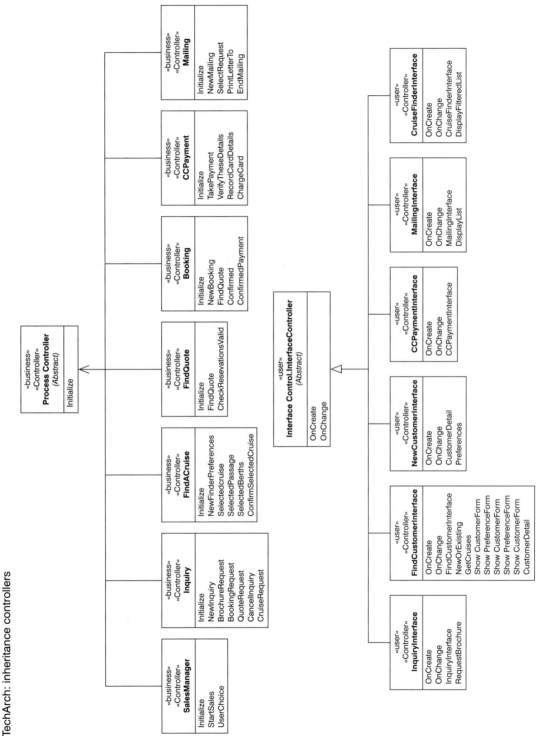

FindCustomerInterface

Figure A20
Controller: Find
Customer Interface

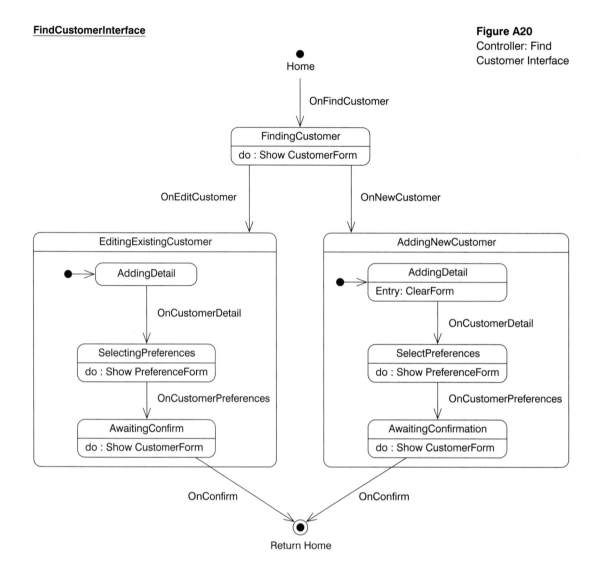

Solution delivery

The use case object sequence diagrams are refined to include the user interface design for the specific solution. First, class diagrams (Figures A21–A25) are developed to define the process/workflow control objects and the interface control objects, plus their inheritance/reuse from technical architecture. Also, state diagrams are developed to specify the page navigation sequence; this is done for each use case, although only a sample is provided below.

Figure A21
Solution: Make an Inquiry

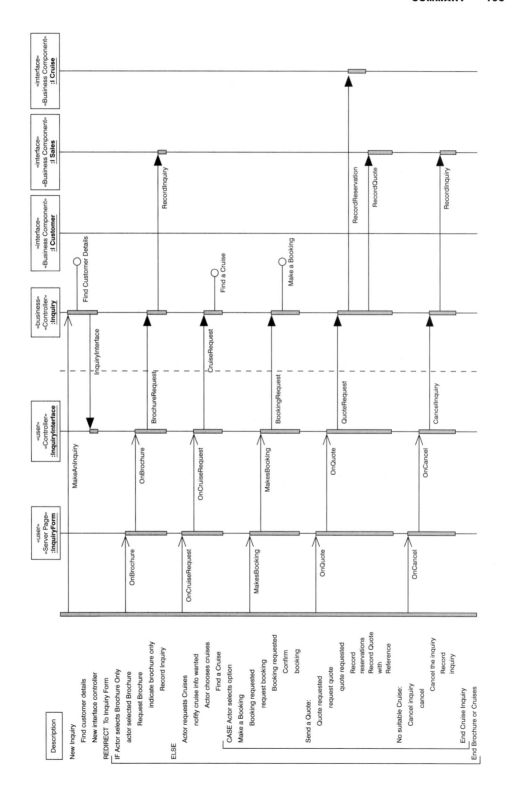

Figure A22
Solution: Find Customer Details

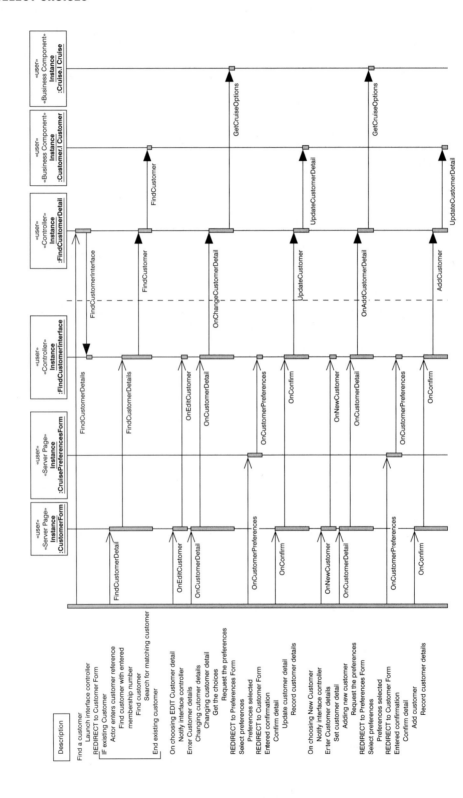

Figure A23
Solution: Find a Cruise

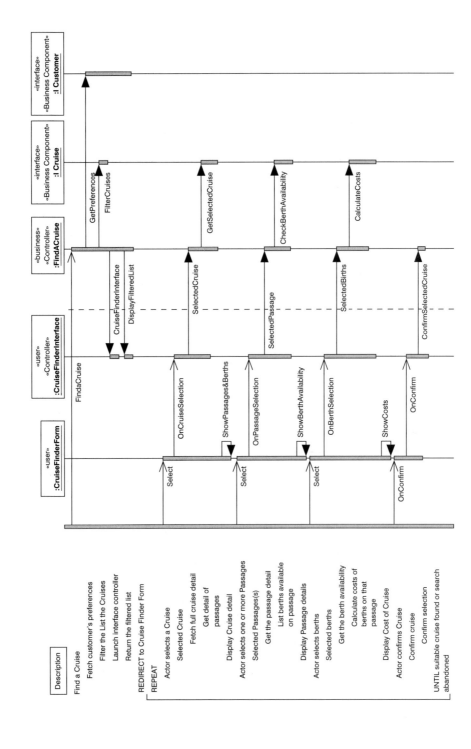

Figure A24
Solution: Make a Booking

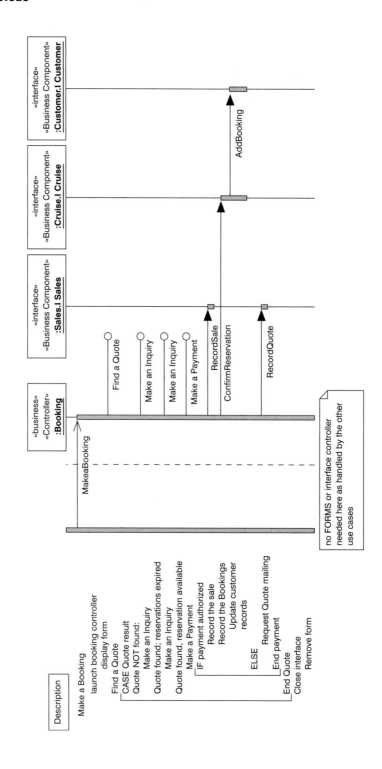

Figure A25
Solution: Send Mailing

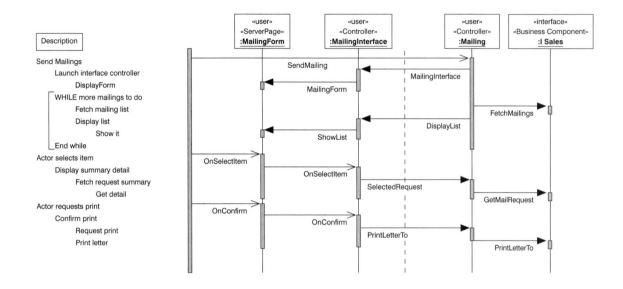

Component delivery

From the 'black-box' specification delivered from the business architecture, component delivery deals with the component and service internal design, leveraging UML to design the internal implementation of the components and services, using new build, reuse of existing assets/components, and/or harvesting of legacy data and functionality.

The internal design encompasses two main UML techniques (Figures A26–A32), internal component class modeling and internal service interaction modeling. The services modeling is prioritized in alignment with the service use on use cases, and their own priority for delivery.

The technical architecture will constrain component design, ensuring 'well-behaved' components. In Select Cruises, data objects provide access to the data tier; these are closely coupled to business objects and provide data transparency to their associated business object. The technical architecture detail can be found in the full case study.

Figure A26
Sales component

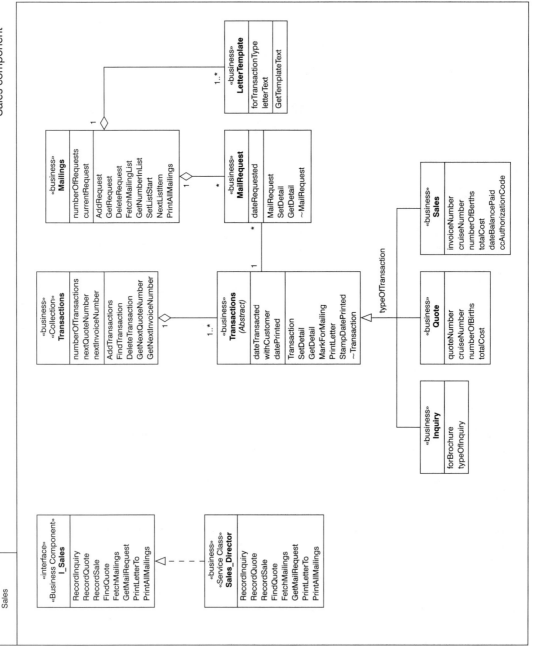

Figure A27
Cruise component

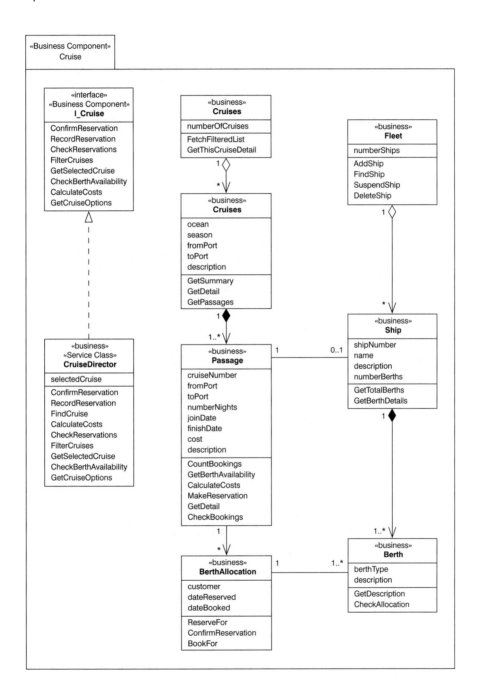

Figure A28
Customer component

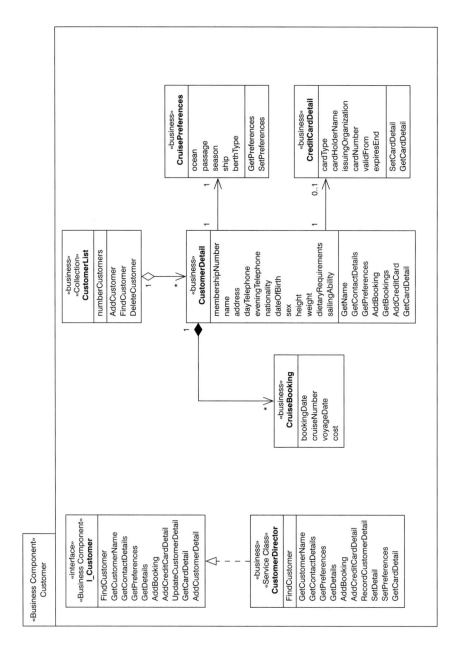

Figure A29
Service: RecordQuote

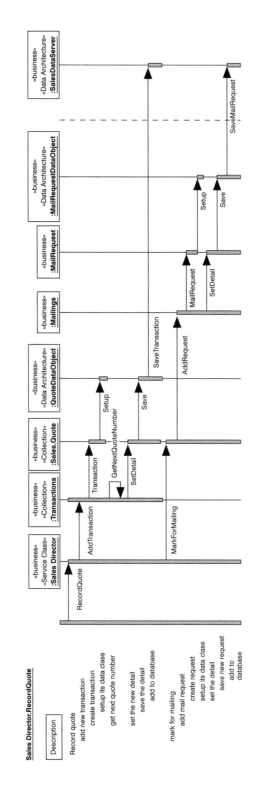

Figure A30
Service: RecordInquiry

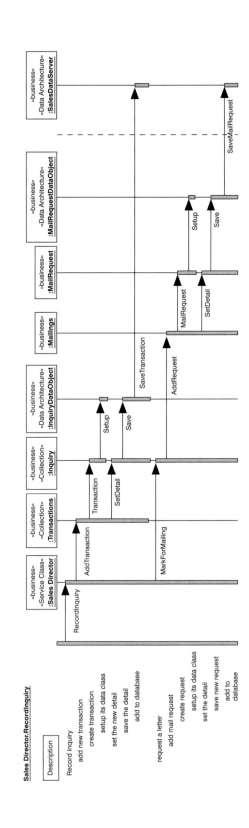

Sales Director.RecordInquiry

Description

Record inquiry
add new transaction
setup its data class
set the new detail
add to database

request a letter
add mail request
create request
setup its data class
set the detail
save new request
add to
database

Figure A31
Service: RecordSale

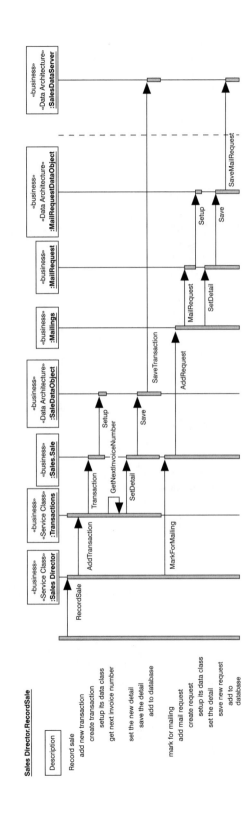

Figure A32
Service: FindQuote

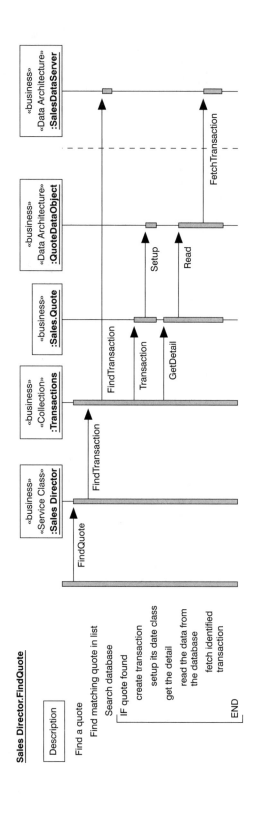

Sales Director.FindQuote

| Description |

Find a quote
   Find matching quote in list
      Search database
      IF quote found
         create transaction
         setup its date class
         get the detail
         read the data from
         the database
           fetch identified
           transaction
   END

Summary

This case study provides examples of the core modeling deliverables within Select Perspective and its workflows that implement the supply, manage and consume paradigm for solution, component and service delivery in contemporary software development and architecture.

Aonix has many years of experience in modeling service- and component-based solutions for all industry sectors, and this case study represents the current best practices for leveragin the power of business process modeling, UML, and data modeling for these solutions.

The diagrams and dictionary definitions are *partial* extracts from the Select Cruises case study; complete examples can be found on www.selectbs.com.

Index